"WHERE ARE THEY NOW?"

We follow a few individuals into the afterlife

Bill Dinkins

Copyright © 2024 Bill Dinkins
All rights reserved.

TABLE OF CONTENTS

Introduction		v
Introduction	"It starts with Frank"	xi
Chapter 1	The growing up process begins.	1
Chapter 2	"There is nothing more important than a Girlfriend, right?"	6
Chapter 3	"I built on the Wrong Foundation."	18
Chapter 4	"Grasping for God"	25
Chapter 5	Moving in with my estranged mom	34
Chapter 6	36 years later "Oh Fudge"	42
Chapter 7	"Precious in the eyes of the Lord is the death of one of his saints."	52
Chapter 8	"Charles dies at the crash site"	58
Chapter 9	"Back above ground, on the Hill"	62
Chapter 10	"Jack and Sophia leave this life."	69
Chapter 11	"Search and Rescue"	76
Chapter 12	"Back to the land of the living"	78
Chapter 13	"He lives, Jack comes back from the pit"	80
Chapter 14	Frank's Body	87
Chapter 15	"Frank and Jack start sharing."	91

Chapter 16	"Frank and Jack catch up".	95
Chapter 17	"The flash back"	105
Chapter 18	"Franks back"	108
Chapter 19	"Make an eternal difference."	110
Chapter 20	"Frank's message at a church"	113
Chapter 21	Sermon day	122
Chapter 22	Jack's sermon	138
Chapter 23	"Construction chaos"	154
Chapter 24	Teeter tottering; between Eternal Life and Eternal Death.	158
Chapter 25	The rest of the story.	165
Chapter 26	Alice returns	168
Chapter 27	Wrapping it up, or not.	173
Last words		187
The Truth Waterfall		191

INTRODUCTION

This may seem unusual to talk with an audience or readers about a story before the story starts. I want all those listening or reading to mull over an incredible event that is happening daily. It's a real event more exciting than any super hero or space movie. It's going to happen to your friends and family members. It's even going to happen someday to you. Someday you will experience an event more exciting than any movie you have ever watched. Unfortunately, for the majority of people it will be scarier than any horror movie you have ever watched. For many it will be a deeper love story than you have ever read or even experienced. It is happening to someone at this very moment. It's happening at almost two times per second worldwide. These very real, permanent, and eternal experiences are happening at a rate of nearly 7,000 times per hour. Again, nearly two times per second. On average it happens over 160,000 times per day on planet Earth. Again, someday this event will even happen to me and you. I'm talking of course about human death. You know, not talking about it does not mean it won't happen to you. In the movie "Where are they Now?' we follow a few people who die. We follow a few people at death; we follow those same people through the doorway of death to the afterlife. This eye witnessed process and event has already been recorded by thousands of people who have clinically died and then been resuscitated. Many come back to life by auto resuscitation. That means no person is actively working on them being resuscitated. It happens apart from outside human help. They come back to life sometimes hours after they were pronounced dead.

When I watch "The Passion of the Christ" I make myself watch all the scenes of the movie. In real life, Jesus received even worse physical treatment than the movie depicted. During the unfolding of "where are they now?' Try not looking away when the intensity of Heaven is being shown. Try making yourself also watch during some of the horrors of a non-born again unbelievers experience. It's important to know what is sincerely going on. We do our best to be accurate, not embellishing either Heaven or Hades. In reality those very real, physical places will be much better and much worse than we depict.

During this movie or story we get several deep dives into what real NDE or Near Death Experience is. We will experience it along side of those that have died. It's important for everyone to be ready for the afterlife. I don't want to be macabre but it is going to happen to us all. As the saying goes "we are either going to God or he is coming for us at the Rapture. One way or the other we will be in front of God." The people we follow talk about their own life and death experiences.

As the story unfolds if you question your own future after you die, go to our website. We can help you connect to Christ and a local church. Lastly be informed and aware

"Where are they now?"

that God loves and get this, God likes you. He has made a way for you to have fellowship with him. Part of your soul is encouraged by that. Another part of you may be scared and push God away. It's normal to shrink away from his magnificent presence. The Bible even says no man can even see God and live. Just thinking about being in a relationship with God can be very scary. Yet fellowship with him is the very reason he created us. It's the giant missing piece of all of mankind's heart. When humans say there must be more to life. They are right. When you have an active, living relationship with the creator who formed you in your mother's womb, your life is larger and more fulfilling than you ever thought possible. God will complete you like nothing or no one else can ever do. Even as I speak, I can almost hear the song covered by Carrie Underwood "How Great thou art" playing.

The single God head of Christ, the Father and the Holy Spirit are worthy of any praise and adoration. Your heart will rise as you offer God love and praise. To resist that is to have your life be small and unfulfilling.

Here is a little background information. I came to write this story after years of seemingly little information about the truth of what is happening to millions of people who die each year. In 2022 more than 60 million people died on planet earth. That has affected many of the remaining living in hard and sad ways. But the other thing to ask and think on is "Where are those 60 million dead souls NOW. In the following year 2023 alone, over 61 million more people died. It's been estimated 40 to over 100 billion people have lived and died on planet Earth. That's if we have been here say 10,000 years or less. What if they did not cease to exist as some believe or they did not come back as other humans or as some random animal.

For many a discussion about death is seemingly "pointless" and scary. Since death is coming for and awaiting us all. Logically, we need to make sure we get it right. As Blaze Pascal said "We are better off to believe in God and see how to get right with him. Than to not believe in God and then see that we were mistaken". This teaching is from the same person who invented Calculus. In this story of "Where are they Now?' we want to demonstrate and remind all listeners, that life is short and eternity is long. It's not just long, but eternal, never ending. Many, many doctors worldwide have witnessed testimonies of their dying patients. Some are favorable near death experiences. Unfortunately the majority of Near Death Experience's or NDE's are not favorable experiences. We will explain why we don't hear more of the negative NDE's during the story.

As we will unfold during this story, many people think and say "I will get right with God at the 11th hour, only then to die at 10:30.

So many people want to have a big exciting life. A life like the heroes we see in movies and print. Your life if you are a Christian, if it is not already, will be unfathomable, beyond words at your death. Being in fellowship with God and other believers will be more fulfilling than your mind can conceive. After the resurrection, Philippians 3:21 your body will be the same that Jesus currently has. As the scripture says "our bodies will be fashioned after his glorious resurrection body." After Christ's resurrection, he had a solid tangible body and he was able to go through solid walls. Jesus and even we in our future resurrected, physical

"Where are they now?"

bodies likewise, will then be able to travel at the speed of thought. Jesus went across lakes, into closed locked rooms. He even went into the sky with his physical body, another words flight.

Enjoy the story after the main story there is brief witnessing testimony. You win some and I lost some. As the saying goes "you miss 100% of what you don't shoot for. I pray it encourages and challenges your soul. James 4:8 "Draw or pull close to God and he will draw or pull you close to him."

Don't be discouraged but feel a sense of brotherhood by this next statement. Jesus said "be of good cheer, if they hate me, they will hate you. Let not your heart be troubled, the world WILL BE AGAINST *YOU!* But I (Jesus) have overcome the world."

Thank you
Bill Dinkins

Book manuscript to become Screen Play

INTRODUCTION

"IT STARTS WITH FRANK"

The year was 2020. In the United States the economy was booming. Much of the world was thriving. That year was starting to get the nickname the "roaring twenties" It was looking like 2020 would be like the roaring economy of the 1920's. From 1920 to 1929 the U.S. had experienced a rapidly growing economy. It had continued until a terrible, financially devastating time period called the "The Great Depression" began.

In the present I'm introducing myself, my name is Frank Locksley. I'm an older aged man I'm thriving in the 2020 economy. I'm a realtor in a hot and happening real estate market. I'm selling homes for record prices. I'm not in Las Vegas. I'm in the more expensive northern Nevada, Reno area. As a realtor for the last seven years I have been enjoying some fair financial success. I even took up a child hood past time. I and some of my brokerage buddies joined other realtors in playing on team in a northern Nevada softball league.

One evening I was relaxing, sitting in my recliner. I was thinking about my upcoming game with a Carson City team of realtors. It was a few days off.

During the next couple of days I intermittently started thinking about softball. It reminded me of little league baseball. I had played baseball as a kid. I started thinking of the many events of my childhood. I started to remember when I was a 10 year old kid. Aw that was a good time all right, I sat there thinking about when I was that age and would hit a baseball farther than any of my teammates. My hits were over the outfield fence. There was one problem; those hits over the fence, those very same hits were always fouls. I mean every time!

I played baseball in little league for three years. I never once hit a homerun. I only had small base hits or over the fence homeruns that were always fouls. For those three years neither my dad nor my step mom ever came to one of my baseball games. Neither did my mom nor my step dad ever attend one of my games. Not once.

Now that I had thought of my little league baseball experience, the memory flood gates opened. For the next several hours I began thinking of all of my childhood and adolescence experiences. Both bad and good ones, I thought first about starting the first grade.

I started the first grade when I was 5 years old. My mother walked me to school that first day. That would be the last day she would ever take me to school. I lived with my mom and step dad from 1st through the end of the 4th grade.

At the end of the fourth grade, my dad wanted me to live with him. My dad mostly wanted me with him because

"Where are they now?"

I had started signing my last name using my step dad's last name. I was growing closer to my step dad. I began living with my dad and step mom during the week. Then I spent the weekends at my mom's and step dad's house. I lived with this arraignment from 5th grade though the beginning of my sophomore high school year.

I did fair in school. I did great in math and science.

I do remember almost always feeling like an inconvenience to my parents. Several times I had overheard my parents arguing about who would take me to the other parent's home for the weekend or back home for the weekdays. My divorced parents were less than thrilled to be my driver. They drove me back and forth twice weekly from the age of 5 until the age of 12

I later found out my grandmother had raised me from shortly after birth until I was four years old. Wrong or right, I came to the conclusion that I was an inconvenience and unwanted by my parents.

When I was in my teens I found out that my mother had discovered my dad was cheating on her. My mom got pregnant with me to 'save" the marriage. Unfortunately my parents were divorced before I was born. My dad's interest was on the other women. My mom was not interested in being a mom to a child she did not want. Until I was in my late teens, I could not ever remember my mother saying that she loved me.

I began to think, "All I need is love". That became a driving desire to me during my high school years. Back at the age of about 12 I asked my parents for a cat. There was a stray Russian blue cat that started hanging out around our home. We started feeding it and then it sort of became ours. We had it about a year and then it got feline leukemia. I was devastated by the loss of that cat it was more than a pet to me. It accepted me. It would meet me as I walked towards home from school. It hung out in my room. It curled up at the foot of my bed at night. This meant a lot to lonely unloved boy. We named the cat Smoky because of blue coloring. After Smoky died, I begged my dad and step mom for another cat. This time we went to the animal shelter and got a blue Russian kitten. I named the new kitten Smoky as well. Quickly that cat became just as wonderful as the first Smoky. Though out the next 40 years I would have at least one cat at all times. As an adult I also had a couple of very special, feisty dogs. They were Shiba Inu's a unique Japanese dog.

Before I hit you with more heavy stuff let's look at some of my lighter memories. It is the memories that you look back on and Think "ah I remember that. That was fun"

I did have many fun memories of being a child;

I do remember many good times as well. "I remembered my Green Machine. It was like a big wheel. But, it was even longer and lower, it was cool for an eight year old boy. I remembered being an insecure boy and then riding my Green Machine to the new neighbor's house. They had moved next door. There were five kids. I had not met the new kids yet. It was 1974 they had moved into the house several days earlier. Back then kids rode these things called bikes. You peddled them. If you don't know what peddling is have an older person catch you up. Oh and many, many kids walked to school. They even walked back home. Now a day's it is considered child neglect to let your kids walk to and from school. Walking a mile back and forth to the store would mean you were a neglected child. In my case I was. I just did not know it. We kids even did things like walk a mile to the grocery store. And get this, we walked back. It was even uphill coming home. I know right? It was not even considered child abuse or neglect."

I remember another fun thing I did while I was in middle school. I had a mile long walk to and the same distance back home from school. Half of the walk was in a field. When I would walk home I would pretend I was a giant robot. More like a walking robot shaped city. Thousands of people lived in this city. It was fun and weird. But what's a lonely boy to do. I was the main hero all the time in this city. I saved the city from giant rocks. I had a dialog in my head. I would make up some challenge to the city, like rain or snow. Or the robot was running out of energy. Since I lived a couple of hundred feet above the field, there was always some type of slipping. The city was always in danger. I did that fun, silly activity for a couple of years. I did that when I walked back and forth from middle school to my home.

CHAPTER 1

THE GROWING UP PROCESS BEGINS.

I graduated from high school, my parents had not. My dad had his own small grocery store. It was a 24-hour a day business. It was a narrow old building in downtown Reno. Gaming was thriving in downtown Reno in 1978. Across the street from his store was a new 13 story hotel casino. It was busy and my dad's old store was now much busier. The store was in a building that was 70 years old in 1978. The store had a full basement. I had to bring cases of soda and beer up the stair case daily. One of my favorite memories was testing how much I could carry. I would carry as many as six cases of 24 ct soda up the stairs. I felt very strong. I also did more and more tasks for the nearly five years I worked there for my Dad. My dad was a produce manger before owning this store. So for a small store we had a lot of very nice produce. Many small bodega's/grocery stores had little or no produce. I learned how to cut cantaloupes and watermelons into smaller sections. Then I added a spoon and wrapped them to sell. In five years I learned almost every aspect of operating a grocery store." This was the start of my nearly 28 years of retail experience.

I also remember meeting two celebrities. One was a local, a man named Mills Lane. He was friendly, and also no-nonsense. He had a law office nearby. He would come into our store sometimes daily to buy a banana and small round glass bottle of Martinelli's apple juice. He was nice to me as a kid. He always visited with my dad. I slowly learned his was a lawyer then became the Washoe County District Attorney. He was a former boxer and a world famous boxing referee. The other famous person I met was Stephanie Zimbalist. She came into the store. I was blown away because I had developed a crush on her while watching a TV show called. "Remington Steel" I approached her and said "you are from Remington Steel." She said "yes I am" I told her I really liked the show and then asked if I could have her autograph. I quickly grabbed a note pad and she happily signed her name. I did not know how to have a conversation fluently with an adult at the time. So after an awkward moment or two she said "it was nice to meet you." I said thank you and proceeded to be star struck while she shopped our little store. She was here in Reno to visit and help a sick family member. She purchased so many items that my dad and I offered to have me help her carry them. She happily accepted the offer. So I carried her grocery bags a couple of blocks. It was surreal walking with a celebrity. I dropped them off at her building. That was it. That was a cool experience for an 11 year old boy.

Another fond memory of mine from that same time was Jai Alai. My dad was born in North Carolina. When he was about 18 he and my mom moved to Miami Fl. They

"*Where are they now?*"

both lived there the next 10 years. During that time my dad became enamored with Jai Alai. He liked the game but he was also a gambler. He also liked and bet on horse and dog races. To this day Jai Alai is the fastest ball game in the World.

In 1978 while living in Reno the MGM Grand Casino opened. At the time it was the largest casino in the world. It was 100,000 sq feet. It also brought Jai Alai to Reno. My dad was very excited. He was excited to be able to see the game in person. He also started taking me to see the games. My dad, step mom and I would go to see the Jai Alai games usually twice a week. I got to where I really liked watching the game. After a year of watching it with my dad, I told my dad "I would like to play the game"

My dad and I thought that sounded cool. Neither of us knew if there was a way for me to ever play. I came home from school one day. I went down stairs to my bedroom. There lying on my bed was my cat of course and something new, a Cesta. That's the wicker "thrower" for Jai Alai. That was the main equipment a person needed to play the game. Seeing it was very cool. This was in the day when cell phones did not exist. I could not call anyone and ask where it came from. Several hours later my dad came home. He asked me "did you see it?" I said did you mean the Jai Alai basket on my bed? He said "Oh you did, it's actually called a Cesta." "It's cool" I said. Then my dad continued, Last night your uncle and I were gambling at the MGM. We were playing 21. At the 21 table was a man with Cesta down by his feet. I asked Him if he played Jai Alai. He said yes. I asked him if he would sell the Cesta. He sold it to me. We kept playing 21. I told the man "my son would like to play. It's too bad kids can't play." I chimed in, "Yah that does stink." My dad then half smiled. Well the player said they had a kids league that play on Saturday mornings. My heart started pounding. "Do you mean I can play Jai Alai, I asked my dad." My dad answered, "Yes you can start leaning to throw and catch. Then practice with other kids." A week or two later I was signed up to learn Jai Alai. I did not make any friends there. I just got dropped off went in to learn and practice. Then one of either my step mom or dad would pick me up. Jai Alai was fun. It lasted about two years and then we were told Jai Alai would be leaving Reno. The league had been hoping to develop professional level players. No one had yet risen to the level of a successful amateur. Additionally the betting on the professional players was not making the MGM enough money. It was not profitable. The game lasted a bit longer at the Las Vegas MGM. The game was there for 7 years. Then it was also terminated. The Jai Alai Fronton in Reno has been part of the hotel convention center space now for the last 43 years. Back in 1980 I was sad about not playing the game. Now it's a happy memory. "I could have been a contender. I could have played pro." Not really.

"Where are they now?"

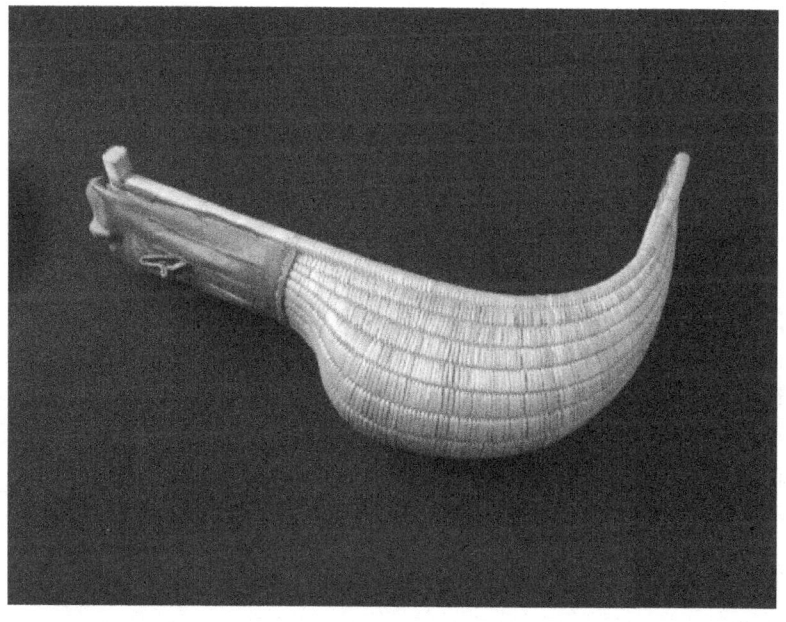

CHAPTER 2

"THERE IS NOTHING MORE IMPORTANT THAN A GIRLFRIEND, RIGHT?"

I started working at my dad's small grocery store on the weekends when I was 11 years old. When I graduated from high school, my dad sold the business. So I worked for the new owner. The new owner was my uncle. I worked for my uncle for less than three months. My uncle started having me work the graveyard shift. At 18 I was not interested in working that graveyard shift. Additionally all the employees had to take a polygraph tests. The polygraph tests happened twice in three months.

This added to my feelings of insecurity. I thought "I need a different job" So I got hired on with a large grocery store chain.

I felt proud of myself. I applied using a paper application; the store manager told me "we have over 3,000 applications." My brother-in-law told me: "Go to the store every day" "Keep checking on YOUR job". I went to the store and also to the district human resource manager for six days a week. I did that for two weeks. After two weeks of that

"Where are they now?"

persistence, the store manager told me. "We have a courtesy clerk position available. It's yours if you want it". I grabbed his hand, and shook it. "Thank you, I'll take the job". The manager told me it's only part time" and "It will take probably a year or more before you can become a grocery clerk."

I worked harder than most of the other courtesy clerks. I ran for price checks, I brought in carts when I was scheduled to. Many other courtesy clerks just sat in their cars or goofed off. I faced up displays, bagged fast for the cashers. I ran quickly from one check stand to another. I said yes to any additional shifts I was offered. I was determined to get as many hours a week as I could. When I had first started I was told I would be averaging 12 to 15 hours per week. After three weeks I was working up to nearly 40 hours a week.

When I first started I was also told it takes approximately one year to be promoted to the position of grocery clerk. A grocery clerk is some one who is a cashier's and stocks shelves. After just two months I was promoted to a grocery clerk.

The other courtesy clerks were jealous and a little ticked.

I was having success at this new job. Yet, I was feeling more and more that now I needed some to love, someone to love me. "Ah ha" I thought a girlfriend is the answer to my loneliness problem. I felt lonely and a little desperate to have a girlfriend. When I thought about having a girlfriend, I noticed something. Out of the blue my blue Russian cat was becoming more like my friend than a pet. As I would notice over the next 40 years that cats and dogs love on us. Many times it's most noticeable when we experience lonely times in our lives. I completely now believe that God does that to help show us love when we may need it most. Not that God wishes us to have animal love more than human love. Sometimes there is a shortage of caring human love. God may want us to feel some kind of love. He may send a caring animal our way. Several theologians have stated this very belief. They have seen it in their own lives and the lives of others. As one child put it, when he was hearing a thunderstorm, he said, daddy I need you. The little boy's father said son God is with us. God is there in your room to comfort you. Daddy I need God with skin on. The boy's father went and held the little boy. Sometimes knowing God loves us seems like not enough. We want someone to hold us. That may even come as a gentle dog looking at us, or lying next to or on our feet. I've had several cats that will reach up with one of their paws to tap me on the face.

On Valentine's Day of 1986 while I was at work, in walked my roommate and a cute young lady. The two walked around shopping a little. After maybe 15 minutes the two came up to my register with two packs of wine coolers and some snacks. It was against company policy to check out or ring up friends. So I had another grocery clerk ring up my roommate. I had no idea who this girl was. I chatted with the girl and my roommate for a few minutes. For some reason I was feeling smitten by my roommate Tom's date. I noticed at the store the girl was talking more to me than to Tom my roommate.

The next day I asked my roommate who was your date? My roommate, Tom said she's just a girl I have sex with. I asked; she's not your girl friend? Tom said, "No, you know I'm dating Chris." I was shocked. Tom went on to say "that girl and I are friends and nothing more."

"Where are they now?"

I guardedly said, "I feel like I clicked with her in just the few minutes you were in the store last night." Tom said, "go for it, I already have a girlfriend, Seriously, I don't want her to be my girlfriend." Tom gave me Karen's phone number; I worked up the courage to call her. I made small talk on the phone with Karen. Then after several minutes of both I and Karen talking, I asked Karen out. Karen said "yes, we can go on a date."

I was on cloud nine. I admit I was a nice looking guy. Yet I had never been on a date as a teenager. I'm 19 now, and am feeling left behind that I did not have a girlfriend. I admit I had built up in my mind that a girlfriend would fill the emptiness that I had. I tried to keep my desperate feelings undercover. I was aware that I was desperate. I knew that desperation would be a relationship killer. I was determined not to lose or run off Karen. It meant too much to me not to be alone.

The two of us went out for coffee. Karen and I spent the next two weeks together. We would see each other every day. I put lots of points in the "love bank" with Karen. To me, Karen was very special and her smile and touch brought me so much joy and acceptance. To Karen, I was a nice guy who liked her.

I was falling in love with this girl. I was 19 she was the "old woman" of 20 years old. There were several signs that this was an imbalanced relationship. It was my first relationship. I had not seen a healthy example from my divorced parents. My friends had single parents. One group of my friend's parents had a long term, yet super dysfunctional marriage. I did not have available a visible model of a healthy relationship.

Karen really, really liked me. She was not in love with me. I started spending all of my free time with Karen. She didn't drive. I did, so I quickly became her ride to everything. I did have a full time job.

If she called I would do everything I could to help her. My friends, family and co-workers said, "Frank that's a problem" I would say "yah but she really likes me". I loved her positive attention. After a few weeks we were starting to have sex. So I thought "I'll do anything for her" To me it meant we were in love. I told myself and believed that this was love. I think to Karen she was in what could be called a "strong like of me". One thing that bothered me was that Karen would not say that I was her boyfriend. On a couple of occasions I would introduce her to someone. I would say, "This is Karen, my girlfriend" Karen would interrupt and say, "No, I'm not his and he's not mine." Hurt and angry I would ask, "What do you mean?" She would gently touch my arm and hold my hand. She would say, "We are better than boyfriend and girl friend. We are best friends." I felt like she meant it. I did feel so close to her. She felt very close to me. So that was enough for me. But we were not doing life together. I gave most of my time, money, and energy, care and concern to Karen. At some point she may have loved me. It was just not the same way I loved her. To me this was enough since I had almost no relationship with any of my family. The few friends that I did have, from them I was slowly isolating myself away from. "I thought it's worth it." "They will always be my friends."

This lopsided relationship continued. For six weeks we saw or talked to each other every day. Then, I felt a distance.

"Where are they now?"

One day I called Karen, several times and Karen did not answer.
These were the days before cell phones.
A whole day came and went with no call from Karen. I drove over to Karen's house. I knocked and finally Karen's younger teenage brother answered the door. "Is Karen here? I asked. "No man" her brother answered. "But I'll tell her you came by." I asked, "Do you know where she is?" Her brother answered, "Well, she's at a friend's house." "Okay, it's just weird she did not call me all day. I was worried about her." On top of that I was insecure and did not know how to handle not being or talking with Karen.

So I went home. I was assuming Karen would call that night. There was no call. The next morning came and no call. No call through out the day. That evening I drove back over to her house.

I composed myself; I did not want to appear jealous. I knocked on her door. Slowly Karen's mom came to the door. "Hi Frank, it's nice to see you" Thank you, it's nice to see you too. Is Karen here?" "No, but I'll tell her you came by." I stood there looking bewildered. "Don't worry she's got your messages, she will call you soon" Karen's mother said. I asked, "Where is she? We usually talk on the phone at least once a day." "I know she's coming home tonight" Karen's mother said. Just then Karen's brother interrupted and said "she's down at the little casino bar with her friend"

I was feeling mad, yet I did not verbally share that with Karen's mom and brother. I said "Thanks, I'll talk to her later". I thought to myself; "I'm going to go find her at this casino bar." I could tell I was I going to act like a weenie. I know, I was so insecure.

I drove a couple of miles. Parked my truck at the casino and went in, I'm only 19 and I look like I'm 15. I see Karen sitting at the bar. I'm feeling ticked and relived at the same time. I had never been to a bar with Karen, or by myself.

Security quickly comes up to me asking for ID. The casino policy is to escort miners off the property. I yelled out, "Karen" she turns around and looks at me. Also a skinny, ugly 30-year-old man turns and looks at me.

Karen and the ugly 30-year-old man come over to me. I am jealous but I try to stay cool. Karen asks? "What are you doing here?" I did not want to sound like a jealous jerk. Or get in a fight. So I say the smallest true answer I could think of. "I just wanted to see you and say hi" Karen looked at me like "Yah right" but did not say it. Karen's tall ugly man friend says, "Karen I'll talk to you later." He did not even care that I was there. They give each other a healthy kiss on the mouth. The skinny guy walks back to the bar.

Irritated Karen says "take me home" we drive the 10 minutes back to her house and I drop her off. She is busy telling me off. "Why did you come down here? Don't you trust me? You're such a little boy!" I don't like dating younger men." I just did not say anything. We pulled up to her house and she said, "Aren't you going to say anything." I said, "I'm sorry" Karen got out and slammed the truck door and said, "We are through" I just starred at her and finally yelled "Fine!" I drove off slowly, torn between wanting to talk and fix things with her and thinking, "I don't want this"

I skipped driving home on the freeway that evening. I left the radio off as I drove. I yelled, I cried. I drove in

"Where are they now?"

silence with a blank expression. This is not how I wanted to have a relationship.

The following day I went to work. I had decided not to call Karen that day. I had got in to a pattern of taking Karen to work. I usually picked up Karen from work and then we would spend the rest of the evening together.

The next day early in the morning Karen called me for a ride to work. I let the call go to voice mail. Then I got home after work. There was another call from Karen asking if I could give her a ride home. Again, I just let it go to voice mail.

Karen called several more times. At 10 pm, she called. I answered. "Hello", Karen replied sheepishly "Hi." After a long pause she asked. "Are you mad at me? I missed her yet said nothing. "Why are you calling me? Frank asked "you said yesterday we were through". Karen jumped in "I miss you, I've been sad all day." "Okay" said Frank. Then after a long silence I hung up. I felt hurt and used. A minute later Karen called back. "What?" I snapped. "Did you hang up on me? Karen asked. "Yes I did I don't need to take this garbage from you. I'm not your boyfriend remember?" She said, "You're my best friend" I asked; "What about your friend from last night?" "He's my old boyfriend". I thought this whole conversation is literally making me sick to my stomach.

I asked; "Where were you for two days?" After a long pause Karen answered "With him" I felt knives stab into my heart. Shoved in by Karen, I hung up again. This time I unplugged my landline phone.

Who knows if Karen called anymore? I went to bed easily for once. I felt a little relief of not being under Karen's influence. I felt free. It was a great feeling.

The next day I went to work. I worked 8 to 5 that day. I felt better without Karen, simultaneously I missed her. I also was of tired of her manipulation.

That day I made no calls to her in the morning. Neither did I call Karen on my lunch. After work I went home. My phone rang a few different times. I figured it was Karen. I remembered her saying "were finished." So I didn't answer. This was before cell phones, or caller ID.

The 2nd day I went to work. I was missing Karen, yet I felt good that I wasn't clinging to her emotionally. I worked 9am to 6pm that day. At 10:30 am. My boss said, "Frank you got a call. You never get calls." I know," I replied. At 1pm I got a second call at work. My boss said, "You can take it." I said "No, but thanks boss." He added, "It's a girl and she seems very nice. She seems a little frantic. Are you sure you don't want the call?"

I replied, "I think it's a girl I was seeing who broke up with me. She wouldn't even say we were dating or that I was her boyfriend." My boss said well "relationships are hard". "Yeah they are" I said. With that I got back to building an end cap cookie display.

A little later in my shift, my boss had me work the dairy coolers. At 4:30 I went outside to grab some shopping carts. I then saw Karen at the bottom of the parking lot. She was walking towards the front of the store.

I quickly pushed some shopping carts into the store. I was trying to think about what to say to Karen.

I didn't really have anything to say to her. I liked some of our relationship. I didn't know what type of relationship we had. I resented her not being "all in" on the relationship. Like I felt I had been.

"Where are they now?"

Karen caught sight of me and came over to my check stand.
Karen asked; "hay Frank, what-cha doing"? "Just working" I replied. Then I asked; "Why are you here?" "I hadn't seen or heard from you for several days. You're not answering any of my calls. I miss you and want to talk and hang out with you"
In my mind I was thrilled, flattered and at a loss. I was also at work. Customers and co-workers were starting to watch and listen in.
I said, "I get off 6pm. We can talk then. Karen replied, "That's okay, I'll wait for you to get off work." She patted my arm and she said "I'll wait in your truck" "If you want to, are you sure?" I asked. "Yes I do" she said sweetly. She went and got a small bag of chips and a soda. Paid for them, then she smiled cutely at me. Then Karen walked out to my truck. I watched from my check stand as she walked from the check stand. She walked directly out the door. She went to my truck. Astonished, nervous and excited I just stared at Karen for a moment. She was now sitting in my truck.
Other employees and customers were staring at me. I knew I had an hour and a half longer to work. I needed to go back to my check stand. I continued cashiering, checking out customers. For the next 90 minutes the store was busy. I kept thinking about Karen sitting out in my truck. She was waiting for me. Every once in a while I would look towards the window. Just to confirm that she was still sitting there, waiting for me. She was.
I had never made up with someone before. I had never had a girlfriend before. I had friends that were girls and light flirtations. I was feeling excited about making things

good with Karen. Things were not right from the start with Karen. But I was too inexperienced to know that. I could barely keep cashiering and bagging groceries. Every now and then, I would catch my boss and co-workers staring at me.

6:00 pm finally arrived. I quickly counted out my till. I clocked out and walked out to my truck. But I didn't want to walk too quickly out there. She was still there waiting. I got in and she gave me a nice kiss. Then she asked "what-cha want to do? I said "we'll I'm hungry." "Do you want to get dinner?" she asked.

"First we need to talk. We need to talk about the last few days. We need to talk about your old boyfriend. I mean what are you and I to each other?"

She said in her cute, glib way, "You're my best friend" I felt like she was sincere. Yet, I also was let down by her statement. "You're my best friend too. I'm also attracted to you. I love you like you're my girlfriend. This imbalance does not work for me."

What imbalance? She asked. I answered, "we have this deepening, sweet, growing connection. To me it seems so wonderful. Then to me, I see you as treating it like its no big deal."

It's like the Journey song." "What Journey song?" Karen asked. It's a great song called "Who's Crying Now". The lyrics say, "One love feeds the fire. One heart burns desire" "That's our relationship; it's me giving, caring, doing things for you. It seems like it means much less to you. You don't commit to the relationship like I do. You're not exclusive. You disappear with your ex boyfriend for two days. That was

"Where are they now?"

this week. Then you get mad at me when I found out. What kind of garbage is that?
 I don't date other women." "You can if you want to," replied Karen. I did not know what to think of that statement. Did she really not care if I dated others? Or was this some manipulation tactic of hers. She said "I'm sorry and reached out to hug me. I looked at her surprised. Then I remembered how I liked to be in her arms. So I caved in and hugged her. It was wonderful, like having a battery recharged. We both sincerely enjoyed the moment of tenderness. It put points back in the bank for both of us.
 We mutually pulled apart. Karen had tears. That moved me. I could see and feel that I was important to her. I felt love for her. Karen asked "are you still hungry?" I replied, "Yes ma'am. Karen said, "Let's go to the Gold-n-Silver, coffee shop". "Alright" I said. I started my truck and then we drove away. The Flock of Seagulls song came on my stereo it was the song called "Space Age Love Song. The lyric "I was falling in Love" kept playing. It was wonderful.

CHAPTER 3

"I BUILT ON THE WRONG FOUNDATION."

For the next couple of weeks Karen and my relationship returned to business as usual. We saw each other everyday. We talked on the phone at least once a day.

We now were closer than before. Karen would not call me her boyfriend. Though disappointing it was enough for Me. We had an emotional and physical relationship so I was kind of content. It was better than being alone. Looking back now almost 40 years, I would now say it was NOT better than being alone.

One day I got off work and drove over to Karen's house. Karen knew I was coming over. I pulled up to Karen's house. I got out of my truck. I saw a man coming out of Karen's mom's house. The man and Karen kissed passionately. She hugged and held his hand as they walked to the man's van. At the strange man's van they hugged and passionately kissed again. Then the man drove off.

Karen noticed me and said hello. I said hello, but instead of walking the rest of the way to her house, I stopped. Shook

"Where are they now?"

my head and said I'm going to go. Karen stood looking surprised as I got back in my truck and drove home.

This was the second time I had driven off from Karen's house with my feelings hurt. I was not the sharpest knife in the drawer when it came to understanding women. I drove home quite again, with no radio on. Being alone and quite with your own thoughts was helping me this time. I got home and decided I was okay. My Dad and step mom were on a 6 month trip across the United States. So when I got home I was just home alone. Karen called and got defensive and ticked off at me for not calling her home first before I came by. She began telling me it was my fault that I saw her kiss another man. She explained to me that it was my fault that my feelings were hurt. I had showed up without calling her from work first. I let her rant and then pretended I was now fine with the relationship. I did not know what else to do. I did not know it but my self-esteem was too low to advocate for myself. I was not even sure I was right. Then Karen even said, I told you I'm not your girlfriend. She told me I was her best friend. That statement I believed. That to me would have to be enough. She told me that she loved me that she wanted me in her life. I just drank that up. She was being honest as well. What she held back is she did not want to be exclusive. She loved me and simultaneously liked sleeping with other men on the side. She did not hide those facts.

I drove the seven miles back to Karen's house. I picked her up and took her out for a late dinner. Later we had sex at my parent's house and she spent the night at my house. In fact she stayed there for three days. I was 20 at this time, part of me felt convicted. I should not be sleeping with a woman. I admit I just ignored those thoughts and continued this dysfunctional relationship. I just told myself this is as good as my life can be at this time. I believed that everything was good, close to even perfect between myself and Karen. Doi! Man how I deceived myself.

As you may know by now, I was kidding myself. I didn't even know it. I just thought I was being positive and making it work. Karen always gave me enough truth, to keep me hanging on. I did not have, nor should I say hear the voice of reason saying, "hay wake up, snap out of it. She's using you."

I decided since I was lonely I would just accept Karen. I would forgive her for anything. I also thought "If I can just love her though this, then she will fall in love with me. Someday she will see how much I put up with and that will make her love me." That can work. Sometimes it also may never come to pass. Proving your love for someone will not guarantee they come to feel the same way about you.

About this time a nice girl at my work started talking quite a bit to me. I of course liked the attention. This girl was nice to me; I felt great pleasure in telling Karen about this nice girl named Tina. Tina was gently, sweetly and regularly fluting with me. I quickly noticed how annoyed and jealous Karen became.

Tina and I were talking at work one day. Tina said "I would really like to go to Disneyland this summer. I really don't want to go there by myself. I can afford to go but none of my friends have enough money to pay their share. I thought about it for a day and then the next time we worked together. I said "I can drive and pay for the gas. Then it's easier for your two girlfriends to cover their share". I knew I had changed the nature of casualness between me and

Tina. She would either back out of it. I did however feel that she would like to be with me. It was exciting to have a friendly young women flirt with me. A couple of days later Tina said "let's do it. The four of us will drive to Disneyland. My girlfriends are on board and it will be Fun." Tina and I started talking non-stop about going to Disneyland. The next day when I saw my love but still friend Karen I told her the news. 'Tina, her two friends and I are going to go Disneyland. Surprised, Karen was less than thrilled. She told me "Tina is just jerking you around. She would not really go with you to Disneyland. That would involve at least one or two nights in a motel." "I replied "I and Tina make good money. We can easily afford it. The three girls are going to sleep in one room and I will sleep in my own separate room.

    The next day, Tina and I worked together. Karen who seldom ever come to my job, showed up at my workplace, unannounced. Karen came over to the check stands where Tina and I were cashiering. Karen asked me in front of Tina. "Would you like to go out to dinner tonight?" An instant awkward moment was created. I took the opportunity to clear the air between the three of us. Tina asked me is Karen your girlfriend? Smoothly, I answered, "She's not my mine and I'm not her hers. This was the same answer Karen had stated to others when previously asked about her relationship with me.

    I added yah getting some food after work would be nice." With that Karen smiled, patted my arm, turned around and walked out to the parking lot.

    After Karen left Tina asked "are you sure you two are just friends? She seemed a little ticked when you said; what you said." "I did want to be more than friends but she Karen does not want that. So I'm not her boyfriend." "Okay then," said Tina, "I think our Disneyland trip will be fun, "added Tina. "It will be" I replied.

After work I drove over to Karen's house. Karen's house was actually her mom's home. Karen lived there with her teenage brother and mom. Karen had never met her dad. I knocked on the door and her brother answered the door. He gave me a cheesy smile. Karen's mom also came to the door. "So I hear you're having dinner tonight. What's the occasion?" asked Karen's mother. "No occasion" I answered slowly. The emotional atmosphere in the room was odd. The mom then asked. "Karen said you two were going out on a date. Is that not true? I was even more confused, "No it's just dinner I have to work early in the morning." The brother, mom and I all raised our eyebrows. We all sat down in the living room. A few minutes later Karen walked out of her bedroom. She came into the living room and had dressed up for our casual dinner. The many times in the past Karen had just worn lose comfortable clothing when she was with me. I stood up to greet Karen. She kissed me on the mouth in front of her mom and teenage brother. This was something she had never done before. In fact she had told me many times she did not kiss me on the mouth because we were not in a boyfriend, girlfriend relationship. Karen asked me if I was ready and we left the house for my truck. We walked to my truck and got in on opposite sides. I started the truck and started to drive away. Karen reached out for my hand. This was something she had never done. She and I never held hands. I had tried in the past and she would say "we are not boyfriend, girlfriend." I had given up on holding hands or kissing her. In the past she had proved

"Where are they now?"

to me that we really were just friends. We were Friends who occasionally slept together. The sleeping together was becoming much less often as well.

I did not comment on her kissing and hand holding. I wanted to appear cool. So I made small talk. I asked about her day. I talked a little about my day.

We got out of the truck to go into a coffee shop. She came over to meet me. She usually walked ahead of me. This time she came over and held my hand to walk into the restaurant. I then asked her why all the attention. Karen replied, "I realize you mean a lot to me and I don't want to lose you" I wanting to be calm said. We are friends and you're not going to lose my friendship. You're my best friend too."

For the next week I and Karen spent a lot of time together. We slept together more. Even more importantly to me, was that Karen was now acting as I thought a girlfriend normally acted. We now held hands, kissed in front of other people. She even now sat next to me in my pickup truck. It was like a county song. Sometimes now she was even a little too clingy. To me though this was the fulfillment I wanted. At the end of this week one day at work Tina had some news for me. She told me that her girlfriends could not go on the Disneyland trip. I figured that was Tina's way of getting out of the trip. Then Tina said "I would still like to go. I have never been to Disneyland. Do you still want to go if it is just me and you?" Yes I would, I replied. It will be fun. I've been four times. It's funnier every time I go.

I had a check inside of myself as I said told Tina all of that. Tina hugged me and dragged her hand on my arm as she let go. I felt I like was now doing the wrong thing by accepting both women's attention. I liked it and also felt a little like a dirt bag. A feeling I had not felt before.

After work I drove over to Karen's house as usual. She hugged and kissed me. She sat next to me on the couch. "How was your day? She asked. It was good I replied. "Have you heard from Tina? You have not talked about her for a week or so."

One reason I had not is because Tina was a floating cashier. She worked at six other stores in the area. I was permanent at my store. Tina only came to my store if my store was short staffed.

I told Karen that my day was good. I did say "I saw Tina today." Karen rolled her eyes. How's Tina, "well she said that her friends could not go to Disneyland." "Let me guess" interrupted Karen "so now she can't go." "No actually she asked me if it was okay if just the two of us went," I replied. "Oh she does like you," mumbled Karen. "What did you tell her? Karen asked. "I told her sure, and then I felt like a dirt bag." Karen blurted out "You should have told her I'm your girlfriend." "You have always denied that you were my girlfriend." I stated. "You know I'm your girlfriend, I love you," said Karen. She kissed me; she had never told me that she loved me. For a person to tell me that was like Heaven to me. I was very lonely, and a person telling me that she loved me placed her in an elevated position of importance in my mind. For the next couple of weeks I was consumed with Karen. I could not spend enough time with her. She seemed to feel the same way I did.

CHAPTER 4

"GRASPING FOR GOD"

Another two weeks passed. Neither I nor Karen had ever been married. We were seemingly both falling in love. We did start talking about living together. Even Karen had never lived with a boyfriend. One day after we both had worked we got together. At dinner that evening Karen, said we should get married. I was flattered. Karen said "we should get engaged and then plan a wedding. We should move in together." I was excited that Karen would say that. Inside my mind, I had the good thought, and bad thought thing going on.

I told her "yes we should do that, and I love you." I also thought and had a feeling that I was now going down a wrong path. I ignored this thought. I figured I would make it work out. I figured most people get the jitters to committing to a long term relationship. I thought in order to have a relationship I had to ignore the thoughts of my own doubt.

In summation, at this point I was not a Christian. I had frequent fears of death. I figured there was nothing I could do about those fears. My best friends for a decade had moved almost 900 miles away. My roommate was a nice guy and a decent friend. I was trust worthy and solid. Yet, I was not a Christian. My dad and step mom were on a six month retirement road trip. They were driving around the United States in their new motor home.

This was in the days again when cell phones did not exist. I seldom talked to my dad while they were on the road. I had not lived with my mom for the last ten years. I seldom talked or visited with my mom. My mom was essentially estranged from me. There were no bad feelings between me and my mother. There was just no communication happening between us either.

With all that said I got engaged with no input from my parents or friends. This may not be healthy but to me it did not really matter anyway what my parents said or did. That was not because I disliked or rebelled against them. I just did not have much connection to my parents.

Therefore, to make a long story longer I agreed to be being engaged, and to living together. Karen was the only person I had. I was nineteen and Karen was 20. She was my first girl friend. I found out later I was her 33rd man. Or I could say partner. She had never lived with or been engaged before. I was in a train wreck waiting to happen. Only I did not know that at the time.

A couple of weeks later Karen and I moved in together. That was May 1st 1986. I had only met Karen on February 14th of 1986. We both had jobs and no debt. It was fun shopping for groceries. We both had some furniture. I had a nice 10 year old truck. So hauling furniture was not a problem. Every time we rode together in my truck Karen would slide in to the middle of the truck. We sat directly next to each other as I drove. I felt like a big man, a loved man. In my mind this was the fulfillment of my longings. I still had that nagging fear of death thought floating in the back of my mind. I did not know what to do with that. That had started at maybe the age of 10 and had slowly increased during the next nine years.

Again I did not know how to take care of that. I figured it had something to do with God. But I thought "I will figure it out in the in the future. There is no hurry now. I just need to have a woman who loves me and then later take care of the growing fear of death feeling. How else am I to think?" I did not realize I needed to change the sequence of my priorities. It was odd to me that this fear of death thought was increasing while I was deepening my connection and involvement with Karen.

As many of us have, I had been influenced by the surrounding culture. Part of my culture of course was TV and movies. As a kid I would sneak down stairs every Easter and watch the Ten Commandments. My step dad was a Catholic. When I was a kid, you had to wait for your favorite show to come on the air, in order to watch it. The Ten Commandments was on from 7 pm until 11pm. That was way past my bedtime of 8:00 pm. I would watch the movie by lying on top of the chairs in the dining room. I was under the table so my step dad or mom would not see me watching the movie. The third year in a row, they caught me and sent me to bed.

I felt drawn to God and to the Bible. Neither set of parents talked to me about God. I had the interest in God, but I did not know what to do with that curiosity. As an adult I think all humans have an inborn curiosity for God. I would say many even learn and draw close to him. I also did not know what that meant.

I also was drawn to romance movies. In 1980 I saw the commercial/trailer for the movie "Somewhere in Time." I did not see the movie in theaters. At the time my friends were heavy in to hard rock. I liked rock music as well. I asked my friends "do you guys want to go see this time traveling romance movie?" With blank expressions they were nice but said "not really" I ignored my desire to see the movie. Several months later the movie came out on Showtime. I again was very excited even as a 14 year old boy to see this movie. I set my alarm to see it at 4am on a Saturday. To me as that point in my life this was a life changing movie. I would sift my relationship views though the influence of that movie. "To me" I thought, that movie captured what I wanted a relationship to be like. In the movie "Somewhere in Time" The man leaves his successful writing career. He finds a way to go from 1979 to 1912. He does it to pursue a woman he has not met but he believes she is the love of his life. They meet and there is chemistry between them. He has many sweet, charming lines he gives her. She is a very intelligent top of her skills actress. She delivers many cute and touching lines towards him. He is smitten and in love with her. She falls deeply in love with him. She asks him to marry her. He says "of course, I'll marry you." Then shortly thereafter he is abruptly taken back from 1912 to 1979. That is the crushing part of the movie. He tries to return to her time, and he cannot. He spends close to a week trying to return from the year 1979 to 1912. He is not successful. For that same week he does not eat or drink. Without the presence of this woman who loves him, he has no reason to

"Where are they now?"

care for himself. He dies from dehydration and starvation. He is reunited in the afterlife with his love.

To me as a teenage boy, with my history of being abandoned, that was a kind of love I wanted. Not to die, but to feel that satisfied with the person I loved that nothing was more important. Not even living. That was extreme but who does not want to be loved by someone more than they love life itself. I was determined to have not only someone I loved but someone who loved me that deeply.

Karen's fondness for me was getting deeper. I had some realistic expectations of a relationship. I also had some very unrealistic expectations. I was not aware of that at the time.

Karen and I moved in together, I was determined to make this relationship work. For a month we played house. Both parties cooked and cleaned. We both maintained our jobs. Karen had even picked up a new higher paying job. It was a solid job at the power company. Karen soon wanted to socialize with her co-workers. She asked me to go. I really did not want to. I worked 50 hours a week and did not want more activity or socialization. Karen wanted to do more fun stuff and hang out with her many friends.

Most men by the age of 40 don't have one 3:00 in the morning friend. That's a friend you can call at three am and spill your guts out to.

I had a couple of guy friends. I did not talk much to them about relationship issues. After five weeks of living together, Karen and I began to argue on a regular basis. I tried to not be a jealous jerk. It was okay with me if Karen went out without me. I just did not want to go out every Friday and Saturday evening. Karen yearned to be with her girl and guy friends on her free time.

At the six week point of living together Karen told me that she wanted to break off the engagement. This was a shock to me; I figured we would work though our differences. This crushed me; I started talking at work with my co-workers about Karen. Talking with Karen only led to more fighting. I was very isolated. I started letting my relationship problems and feelings of sadness interfere with my work attitude. I started showing up late to work. I was short with my co-workers. I was getting insubordinate with some management. I was going from an ideal employee of two plus years to a grumpy, sulky, complaining employee.

One Friday evening I was waiting for Karen to come to bed. Even though we were broke up, we slept in the same bed. That was hard, even heart breaking to me. We usually went to bed at the same time. At 10:00 pm I walked out to the living room to see if Karen was okay. She was just watching TV. I asked if she was Okay. She said "I'm fine. Just go to bed." I went back into the bedroom and slowly fell asleep. I was feeling quite sad even despondent about how this broken off engagement was affecting me. I felt like I was starting to die on the inside. I noticed to Karen it had no seemingly negative effects.

At about midnight I woke up again. Again I noticed that Karen had not come to bed yet. I could faintly still hear the TV playing. I also faintly heard talking. The furnace turned on so under cover of the furnace roaring, I quietly opened the bedroom door. I tip toed to the edge of the hallway. Then I quietly peaked around the corner of the living room.

I saw the most heart breaking thing I had ever seen up to that point in my life. I saw Karen on the couch naked with one of her and my friends. I was in disbelief. I was angry and jealous, but that gave way to sad despair. I realized this person who I had put 5 months of my life into was throwing me aside. She was treating and thinking of me as a disposable piece of garbage.

I had come to the conclusion that nothing was more important than love. I even believed that love was stronger than steel. Love was even stronger than death. This love I thought and believed was real and had disappeared. If I just love her though this I thought, then she will come back to me. That may work at some point, but now for me, that was too long and too painful of a game plan. Plus you never know if the person you're holding on to will "wake up" or "come to their senses." I just slowly walked back to bed. I felt like the pain you would feel if someone operated on you if you were awake. This was even worse because her sex with another man was not meant to help me. But it was to dismantle and destroy our relationship. Part of me died a little that terrible evening. It did give me resolve to not live in that apartment anymore. I was not going to let her treat me like that anymore. No matter what I would get free of her. She could go live somewhere else. I would rather be alone than with someone like that.

I became even more dysfunctional at work. Two weeks after the catching her in the act event I was fired from work. I even told Karen the morning after that I had caught her and I that I saw her having sex on the couch." She snapped at me coldly. "Remember we are not engaged now. I can sleep with whoever I please. I have not promised you I would not see other men." She was right, she had not promised that. In point of fact, Karen even wanted us to still live together because she did not want to go back to living with her mom and younger brother. I suppose she also enjoyed the rides and anything else materially she could manipulate from me. I did not want to live with her from that point forward. I was forced to briefly live with her because I had a 6 month lease and could not afford to pay for a separate apartment. She would even tell me "if I was a real friend and if I really loved her I would stick it out until she found another place to live." I was beyond sad and miserable. When I got fired it was a blow and yet I also felt a sense of relief. She said "we can make it work. She really only meant I could get another job and continue to support her in the life that she was accustom to living.

I said "no, I'm going to move out and live with my mom. I need a break from this situation. She was enraged, I did not really care. I could not be around someone I loved and have her think I was just there for her convenience. She asked "what about the lease?" The lease was in my name. I said I will go talk to the leasing office and see if they can let me out of the lease. She said "that's the coward's way out. If you really love me you will keep this place until I have a place to go myself." I said "I can't, I do not have a job and cannot pay the rent on this apartment. For once it felt okay, even good to be broke with no money coming in. I could have jumped into another job. I did not have it in me at the moment to be whole and competent for another job.

I called my mom and asked if I could live with her a short while, just until I got back on my feet. She said that's fine. I begrudgingly moved Karen back to her mom's house. She was swearing and nasty to me the day I drove all her stove

"Where are they now?"

back to her mom's house. I admit I could not wait to stop seeing her every day. The day I moved her stuff back I was not gracious I put her stuff out side at her parent's front gate. I had thrown a few things. At the time it was aggression therapy. I did not really care how or if her stuff was broken or where Karen wanted it.

CHAPTER 5

MOVING IN WITH MY ESTRANGED MOM

I had not really had much of a relationship with my mom from age 10 to 19. After I moved in with my mom my depression set in even more. I still loved Karen, and I was missing her. I was mad at her and growingly even at God. God had done me no wrong. I was just ticked at him. I had really never talked to God in my first 20 years of life. Now he was on my radar. I became more despondent of life. I did not know what to do with my feelings of love and resentment towards Karen. I did not know how to deal with my growing feeling of the fear of death. I felt like I needed to connect with God. But I had no knowledge of how to do something that seemingly odd. I quickly slipped from a healthy 170 lbs down to 125 lbs. I was not dieting. I was losing my will to live. I had come to the conclusion that love was the most important thing in life. And I had lost that love. At this point I immersed myself more into the movie of "Somewhere in Time." I really liked the upbeat music and

"Where are they now?"

indentified also with the sad music and deep despondent loss for the main charter.

One evening in bed I was crying and said to the Lord "please take my life." I was determined not to take my own life. I said "Lord my life, my plans do not work. Lord please take my life and do whatever you want with me." As I was praying that, tears were running down my face. My life felt so empty and seemingly meaningless. In some measures that was true.

If we place and prioritize being with and pleasing God in the "not very important category" We will have major emptiness, even if we fill and cover over that same God created void with friends, family, romantic relationships and material success.

When I prayed sincerely that first time, I had a reassurance that I had never experienced. I knew that God was listening. I had never felt God's presence before. I did not even know that was a possibility. I had a new realization that God was the answer I needed. I still did not know what he was an answer to. Before that day I had thought "What did I need God for?" Looking back I know now, I needed him for everything good in my life.

The next day I talked to one of my friends. I asked him about God. He said you should go talk to the father at our church. I drove to talk to the priest. He was very nice to me. I was talking all over the place. The priest patiently listened to my ramblings. Then he said "you should read this." He then handed me a new testament.

This was the first time in my life I thought "yah I will read the Bible." I was now very drawn to learn what the Bible had to say.

Since I currently had no job I started reading it that same early afternoon. It was a "Good News New Testament" The priest had told me to start with the gospel of John. As I read each sentence the words were cutting me open. I found out later as the Bible says. "God's word is alive and full of power. It's sharper than a two edged sword. Dividing between the soul and the spirit, being a discerner of men's hearts" I felt like the Bible knew me. The Bible and the Holy Spirit were now dismantling my thoughts and feelings. Then I was being put back together stronger, and more solid. To this day, it will still perform that process for all of us. The words in the Bible and the Holy Spirit were performing surgery on my thoughts. The living words was taking captive, incarcerating the destructive thoughts. To quote Yoda, "You must unlearn what you have learned." How many times do we think we have something figured out and then learn later that was not reality? The Bible says "to put on the mind of Christ. The Bible then put life changing truths into my mind. I felt like my mind was starving for and craving the word. The more I read in the many days to come I realized God was very real. Coming to the conclusion God is real and interested in your life is life giving. I realized God loved all of mankind. Sadly a majority of mankind does not love him. I also realized he loved each of us specifically, and individually. He loves each inhabitant of the Earth. Its life changing when each individual soul realizes Christ loves you specifically. Again not everyone experiences that in a personal way. God offers a relationship with himself though the door of himself, paying for your redemption. The majority of mankind says in their own way, "no thank you"

I had wondered up until this point about God, angels, Heaven and Hell. I now know with scholarly clarity they are real. The spirit world is as real as the nose on your face. Someday when you or I die, we will see it in an instant. Its real, it's right here. We may not be tuned in to it. But it is in our immediate presence.

I started to talk to my mom about what I was learning. She would stay up late and watch shows like "Praise the Lord" She would watch the "700 Club" This was a world I had not ever paid attention to before.

After thanksgiving of that same year I was up late reading though the New Testament. I came across the scripture that read "if you confess me before men I will confess you before my Father in Heaven." Then Jesus continued saying "if you will not confess me in front of others I will not confess you in front of the Father." I sat there blankly trying to figure out what that meant. The Holy Spirit convicted me to tell someone, anyone that I had accepted that Christ was the way the truth and the life. I walked quickly out from my bedroom into the living room and told my mom. "Mom I just accepted that Jesus died and was buried. That he rose from the dead. That he is the way the truth and the Life. That he died for me, and I can't make it in this life without him. I can't make it to Heaven in the future without Him. When I did that I felt a peace that I had never known in my life. I felt that God was no longer out to stop me from having fun. I realized that God loved me. That he had made a way for me to be reconciled to him. There were no longer bad feelings between me and God. I realized that the feeling of peace I felt was not just a feeling but a spiritual entity. It was actually the Holy Spirit.

That as you may know is one equal member of the Trinity. It was God himself. This gift of the Holy Spirit is the second birth, it is also known as being Born Again. To be Born Again means the birth of the Holy Spirit coming alongside of a person's soul.

My mom stared at me after my statement. She said "that's great. Sit down here with me and watch this program." I sat there happy to watch a religious program. I was pleased that I had publicly stated my faith in Christ. I had just given a mini one minute sermon.

This all happened to me at the age of 20. My life was never the same from that point. I learned several critical truths at this point in my life. That I had to confess Jesus before others or Christ would not confess or acknowledge me before his father. Jesus said if you're not for me you are against me. I knew I had to tell others that the Holy Spirit was now in me and in my life. Jesus calls this the second birth, meaning the birth of the spirit. This was the oddest yet best event ever. That God was with me. Jesus says "I stand at the door of your heart and knock. To anyone who opens the door. I will come in. I will be with him, and he with me. The Bible also uses the word heart interchangeably with the word mind. God is in your mind, saying I'm here. I'm ready to forgive you, I died for you. I want you with me in spirit. I made you to be connected to me. I am the love of your life. I truly, deeply, passionately honestly love you. I want to call you my friend. I want us to spend time together. I think specifically about you. I made you. I came that you might have life and have it more abundantly. I knew all this and more. I could feel this lover of my soul with me. The Bible says he is in our midst. To those who will not accept him he waits at the door of their mind. Christ stands and speaks in their mind and knocks. They may keep Jesus at arm's length, away from the non believer. That distance between a person and God is up to the person.

At this point in my life when I turned 20 I was alive towards God. I now knew he created this new life in me, I could not. There is not the ability to do so in mankind. I can't make myself a Christian. It's like this; if I go into a garage do I become a car? If I walk into a church do I automatically become a Christian? No, God does the changing, He adds the Holy Spirit along side of us. No human has the ability to do that. God does the changing. Therefore, I should conclude I can't get to Heaven by my good works. I also accept that I am living life to please myself. I must accept that I can't do life correctly without him. Since then I have also learned that before a person becomes a Christian a person is telling God, I don't need or want you. God respects your choice; he will not force himself upon you. The Bible says of becoming a Christian or having the Holy Spirit with you, it's actually your adoption. We are adopted and also grafted into the family of God. We become the bride of Christ. We are also called the friend of God.

With that are also all the benefits of being redeemed, meaning purchased out of the world's system. We are redeemed out of the power of our sinful natures. We still feel the pull of sin in our mind. We are now the called out ones. That is what the word Church means, the "called out" of this world one's. We are pardoned and saved, that's beyond wonderful. I and all Christians are part of a Kingdom, an eternal Kingdom. It is beyond anything we can even think or Hope. I and all the other born of the spirit individuals are literally part of the Kingdom of Heaven, and the Kingdom of Christ. Before I was saved I did not possess any of these real truths and benefits. They were out of reach; they did not belong to me. Heaven is to be with the Lover of our Soul

This is the very book that changed my life

"Where are they now?"

CHAPTER 6

36 YEARS LATER
"OH FUDGE"

Back in the present time, it was the day of the Carson City softball game. Usually we took our own separate cars to the games. Today we rented and I drove a big passenger van. We thought it would be fun to all ride together. There were nine players who could be on the field at once. But there were 14 of us on the team. Our city league softball team was called the "Rock Stars." We got that name because at the time being a realtor in northern Nevada was a good job. Into the huge van, we loaded snacks and softball equipment, ice chests, clothes, music etc.

We had a 45-minute drive from Reno to Carson City. It was a beautiful day. The high was 70. It was sunny and none of the usual notorious daily afternoon winds. It's almost always windy every afternoon in Reno. We drove at a leisurely pace through Washoe Valley. We drove on the old highway on the far west side of the valley. It's a slow drive. In sight were beautiful trees, deer, eagles, and fancy homes as well.

"Where are they now?"

After we got to the field in Carson, we unloaded. We did this weird thing called practice. We usually didn't practice on a game day. As matter of fact we did not practice much on practice days. We chatted and goofed off a lot on practice days. Oddity of oddity we won that game. We did not usually win games.

We were all in good moods so we stopped for lunch at a local Carson City steak house called Red's Old 395 Grill. Many of the other team joined us at the restaurant. As normal it was super good. We had a nice leisurely lunch. Complete with smack talk and mostly just small talk between us all. I ate way more food than normal. It was a lot of fun. It was enjoyable relaxing at the table with co-workers. Some of which were friends. After lunch it was time to head back towards Reno.

We waddled back to the van and headed back to Reno; on the way home we planned to go though Virginia City. From there back home to Reno, we took highway 50 to highway 341. As we drove we saw old mines and homes. It was cool looking at 150 to 200 year old homes and businesses. Some looked beautiful, others okay, and some were literally collapsing shacks.

Our plan was to stop at least, at our two of our favorite spots in Virginia City. That would be the cemetery and Grandma's Fudge Factory. We could even check out a mine on Main Street. It was in the back of a gift shop. We stopped first at the world famous "Grandma's Fudge Factory" It's been open for over 52 years.

All 14 of us got some candy or fudge there. It's great, their fudge does not melt. They have mastered their candy making technique. You get to watch them as they make different flavors of fudges and candy. I promised my three daughters and my wife fudge. At the Fudge Factory I purchased three pounds of fudge to go, I also got 5 caramel apples for the family.

That afternoon the weather was still sunny, warm, no wind, and beautiful. None of us had to rush home. The whole team thought we would look at some of the attractions of Virginia City.

After Grandma's Fudge we went to the Ponderosa Salon. It was not for a drink but for a mine tour. Parts of the main street, in Virginia City backed up to a large mountain. This giant hill has hundreds of miles of mine shafts still in it. Many were dug in the 1860's. The back end of the Ponderosa Salon is attached to a mine. To this day you can tour the mine. We all purchased a ticket and went into the mine. Some of the group changed their mind and stayed in the gift shop and probably at the bar.. The mine goes several hundred feet into the side of the mountain. The tour guide showed us several cool things. Like a powder room. There miners use to keep gunpowder. They used that to break apart rock and dirt. It was quicker than using a pick and shovel. Gunpowder was used in mines before they had dynamite. The tour guide even showed us how to use a hand drill. It was square and flat on the point end. You hit the iron drill bit with a single jack and then lift it up and turn it a quarter turn. That way it would not get wedged or stuck in the rock as you hammered. I remember thinking all of this was cool. Many of the rest of my group were nervous and wanting to get out of there.

While I was looking at the mining tools and other cool items in the mine, I randomly start thinking about Christ.

"*Where are they now?*"

For some reason, on the mine tour my thoughts started to drift, on to spiritual things. I could feel the Holy Spirit's presence. His presence is by far and away the best part of being a Christian. The way God causes his Holy Spirit to live along side of us. Is He does that when we believe and say that Jesus was raised from the dead and resurrected. We confess to others that Jesus is the only way to be saved. We can't earn it. Christ has to get us into Heaven. Without his approval we are not getting in to Heaven. It's a gift of God lest any man should boast. How could being "Good" for 70 or 80 years earn us millions of years' meaning an eternity in Heaven? Mathematically; it cannot. Heaven is a disproportionate benefit. Spending a moment in God's presence is beyond wonderful. Spending forever with him in a perfect environment is far beyond description.

Sheol and the eventual residence of Hell, is also disproportionate. Telling Christ for a lifetime no thank you, I don't need you. That gets the non-believer a withdrawal of all things good, forever. That is a disproportionate terrible loss to the non-believer. Remember Christ, who is God, is the source of all things good. Focus on the word ALL, that is how much good is gone when God removes himself from your presence. ......All!

The Bible says in Ezekiel 33:11 "As surely as I live, declare the Lord, I take NO pleasure in the death of the wicked." I thought about that as the tour guide was telling us of many miners who had died in all the mines up at Virginia City.

I had these thoughts filling my head for a few minutes. I even stopped walking and had a "checked out" look on my face. The group had moved on and I was dragging up the rear. Alice tapped my arm and asked "are you all right, why are you just standing here with that smile and blank look on your face."? "I'm good" I replied.

The whole tour group continued going forward. The tour guide stopped and said "see this door here? Behind that door are two hundred more feet of tunnel and then a 500 ft shaft going down. We are not going that way. As you have noticed the light in here is bright. I will now show you how much light a miner would have had." The tour guide lit a candle and then said "this is how much light a miner had". Then he turned off all the overhead lights and it was very dark. He said this was all the light a miner had. And several times a day an up draft or breeze would blow out your candle. They would even stop burning if you ran out of air. Sometimes the miner would have trouble relighting their candle, because of the lack of oxygen. Our little tour group was a little uncomfortable at this point. At this point the tour group leader said; "now check out how it looks and feels down here when your candle goes out." With that he snuffed the candle light out. We saw and could feel the blackness. It was the kind of pitch black where you cannot see your hand in front of your face. It began to feel paralyzing, a little unnerving.

Some of our group started to mumble, "I don't like this" "turn the lights on" said another" I blurted out "it's okay the guide will turn the lights back on." He said "that's right" With that, the tour group leader turned the mine lights back on. During the next few minutes, I overheard some of our group talking about how awful it was when it was dark. I thought to myself the afterlife for a non-believer is going to be that bad. It will be even much worse. I thought to myself, "Thank you Lord, that because of you, I won't have to experience fear and terror at my death. I kept this thought to myself and we all moved to the exit of the mine tour.

We exited the Ponderosa bar and slowly walked towards our big passenger van. We stopped at a few of the many stores along the way. A few of us picked up souvenirs.

"This has been a nice relaxing day." I told a few of our teammates. Most of the team nodded in approval. We all finally got back to the van. It was still sunny and warm out. I asked "Are you all up to the last stop?" Someone asked me, Frank how long will we be there? I'm not sure, probably an hour, I answered.

We full bellied little piggies; I mean athletes loaded back in to the van. We drove maybe a mile to our last stop of the afternoon. The Virginia City Cemetery, it's an over 160 year old cemetery. It used to be part of 25 cemeteries in Virginia City. It's now known as the Silver Terrace Cemeteries. It has over 4,000 people buried there. There are only 1300 headstones remaining, the rest have been stolen, vandalized, or have decomposed. The old cemetery fascinated many of us. It's somber and there is some southing effect of quietly walking around a cemetery. The fourteen of us felt cathartic as we walked between the headstones. There was lots of small talk between all the members of the group. Death has a way of bringing deep introspection. Deep life and death talk can be unnerving to many. Of course people only go as deep as they are comfortable going. Some of the group seemed untouched by being in a cemetery.

I had been a born again, Christian at this point for 36 years. I think to most Christian's death and the afterlife hold great significance in their minds. To the non-believer it is many times a shunned thought and conversation topic.

While I was walking in the cemetery, the Holy Spirit quickly recalled to mind the scripture that said "to be absent from the body is to be present with the Lord. So as I walked around that cemetery I felt good and bad. I looked at many tombstones. I thought each person here had already decided during their life to either accept Christ's gift of pardon, or to reject it. According to the Bible a larger majority of people think to themselves. I really don't need to be accepted or forgiven by God. I'm not a sinner. I never killed anyone. I never robbed a bank. God has nothing to forgive me for.

I had my afterlife thoughts as I leisurely strolled around. I looked at each tombstone. Thinking "is that person with Christ and his or her saved loved ones? Then I would envision all the joy and fullness of heart they must be experiencing at this very moment. Perhaps they had felt Christ's presence since before the moment they had died, a hundred or more years earlier. That would fill me with joy, hope and peace.

I also thought statistically more of the people here, according to Jesus probably told God, no thank you. I don't need or want your gift of forgiveness. I know that God honors that decision as well. Then I would look at the tombstone. Wondering if the person who had died a hundred or more years ago had gone where there is no good. God is the source of all things good. There are over 70 scriptures stating God is the source of all Good things. For the non-believer at death they cease to be a recipient of all the good things of God. They are now sealed in their state of rejecting Christ. To experience the rejection and wrath of a rejected God is awful. Even here the word awful

"Where are they now?"

is an understatement. Hebrews 10:30-31 says "It is a fearful thing to fall into the hands of the living God." Believe me you want God as the lover of your soul. You don't want his wrath. There is no one who can withstand that.

Then I would think some of these poor souls are in misery. That was a source of great sadness. I would look down and think "Is this person at this very moment in Sheol, also known as Hades. Luke 16:19-31 is a scripture that Jesus told a specific story about two specific people. One is a man called Lazarus and the other is an unnamed rich man. This story is told not as a parable but as a witnessed event. I had this story going thru my mind as I looked at the many headstones. I knew I could not just focus on the spiritual realty of this location. I would switch back to the mindset of being here and in the moment. Thinking and focusing on easier discussion topics.

I switched gears and remembered that I wanted to make a calendar using photos of the tombstones there at Virginia City. I also thought at the moment, the rest of group was not as interested in talking about the afterlife as I was.

I took many photos of the tombstones. I make an annual calendar using family photos. I thought this year I would make a Virginia City tombstone calendar. After about an hour of walking around, and looking at tombstones it was time to go. There could be a short book just on the stories I was hearing from the rest of our group. It would be full of the faces of us as they looked at the children and adult tombstones.

The 14 of us all slowly walked and loaded back into the van. Reno was just 13 miles down the hill. We were making small talk about the game and Grandma's Fudge Factory. I was now thinking about some of my left over rib eye steak and garlic mashed potatoes from lunch. I would gobble that up in the middle of the night. It was a slow relaxing drive down the hill. The views are spectacular while you drive down that hill. You see Mount Rose. You can see maybe 40 miles in different directions.

I was driving slowly and some driver of an old truck came up quickly behind me. He wanted to pass. I kindly gestured to him to let the old truck drive around me. The driver waved as he drove by.

I noticed the old truck bed construction debris. The bed of the truck had mostly old boards in it. I did notice as he drove by that the load was not strapped down. He got way ahead of me and that was the end of that.

There are several tight inside and outside turns as you come down from Virginia City to Reno. I had not seen as the old truck went around one corner that a couple of old boards rolled out of his truck bed. Coming down the long steep winding roads is safe unless you have a flat tire. Let alone if three tires blow out.

That's what happened to us while the stereo was playing "Queens; we are the champions". We came around a corner, and our van hit drove over two old boards and picked up their nails as well. The old boards had big lag bolts attached to them. Neither the passengers nor I saw any of the road debris. Our van hit the bolts and nails. It all happened on the driver's side. Both rear dual tires and the front tire went flat in just a few seconds. The three flats were on the driver's side of the van. The van leaned and pulled very hard to the left.

"Where are they now?"

People in the van started yelling and screaming. The two folks napping stayed napping. The van pulled hard to the left of the single lane road. The van was then clipped on the back driver's side, by a big truck quad cab 4x4.

Getting clipped by the on coming truck, combined with three flats on the drivers side sent the big passenger van towards and crashing over the side of the hill.

It's a 2,000-foot decent from V.C. to Reno. Some of the hills are steep. Our passenger van missed the guardrail, drove directly off the narrow two lane mountain highway. The van rolled and tumbled down several hundred feet of mountain. When the van stopped all the riders were injured. Some were close to death.

CHAPTER 7

"PRECIOUS IN THE EYES OF THE LORD IS THE DEATH OF ONE OF HIS SAINTS."

Psalm 116:15

I was in disbelief; I was trying to figure out what had just happened. I thought, "A few minutes ago we were all enjoying a nice day. People were snaking on fudge. I had even been secretly eating my wife's garlic French fries. The ones I was supposed to give to her with her steak sandwich when I got home. I started to recall what had just happened, I remember driving; we were enjoying the ride home. We were listening to and singing along with "We are the Champions." I remember a nice old man wanted to pass me on the road. I let him pass. A few minutes later I heard a couple of thuds or bangs. I felt a tire go flat and then another". Frank realized "I must have had a flat tire". In fact the van had got three flats in a matter of moments.

"Where are they now?"

I recognized that I was on my side. I was still strapped in with the seat belt. I had turned in my seat, and the van was upside down. "I've been in an accident," I muttered. I noticed I was bleeding heavily at both of my legs.

It was quiet then. Like the quiet you experience on the top of a mountain. When there is no wind or chirping birds. It was so quiet I could hear my heart beating. I was actually very relaxed. I sat there for a few minutes looking at the beautiful view of the huge valley and the snow covered Mount Rose in front of me. I tried to undo the seatbelt but I couldn't. I thought "I might not make it home. In fact I said, "I think I'm dying".

I loved my wife and three daughters. I was overly attached to my two dogs and four cats. My life was full.

I knew that I was not alone. None of the other passengers were seemingly awake. I had become a Christian 36 years earlier. I had felt the Holy Spirit many, thousands of times in my life. When I sinned the fellowship felt distanced. When I confessed that I had sinned I would again experience of the presence of the Holy Spirit. I thought to myself "this is truly a feeling and a peace that is beyond understanding."

I muttered to myself again, "I think I might die up on this mountain." I felt so much comfort, I felt at ease. I was okay, even content. I knew I very much wanted to live and yet I was also ready to die. I knew to not ever think of death was imbalanced. I was okay with the thought of dying. My eyes were still open; yet my focus was not on the beautiful Mountain View. I was growingly aware that an angel and the Holy Spirit were directly next to me. They were becoming visible. I asked, "Who touched me? "I had just felt a pat on my shoulder." I could now see the angel who had touched me. I thought to myself "The decision-making, thinking, emotionally feeling part of me is slipping out of my body". I began to see a light. "As a Christian I had felt the spiritual part of me next to and in God's presence. Yet, I was feeling it much more intensely now."

I knew I was at the doorway, the very threshold of death. I thought, "I've had this same feeling before, that I had felt when I was still in my body." I was now in a more intense presence of the Holy Spirit. Frank said, "The Holy Spirit is surrounding me." I feel like he's holding me. I feel so loved. "It's fantastic." I instantly knew there was no other place I wanted to be." "I was wholly satisfied. Again, the material world was not all I saw. It was still very much there, but fading from my interest. I was not trying to look past it. The beautiful view of the mountain just was not as satisfying to me. It did not fulfill me like now being in God's powerful, forgiving, loving presence.

I thought and felt so deeply that God was satisfying my soul. I was feeling his love for me. That feeling was stronger than any feeling I ever had in my life. I knew that I was home. I was filled with the thought that "I'm where I wanted to be my entire life."

I noticed more angels. I thought to myself, "They actually do have wings. I was surprised by the size of the angels. They are like 15 ft. tall." One angel came over to me. The angel was just smiling at me; I told the angel "I'm soaking all this in." The angel did a smiling head nod. I told the angel "everything is amazing, my mind is so much sharper and faster."

"*Where are they now?*"

My mind saw very little of earth at this point. I was instantly in this new highly intense presence of the Holy Spirit. One moment I was alive. The next I was in God's more intense presence. I had no feeling of traveling to get there. This Heaven reality exists here in our midst. In the same space we now live. We just don't see it. Because the things God has created keep our minds and eyes full all the time. But at death, we are still here on Earth and simultaneously in his now experienced and felt presence.

I also noticed that I could recognize other people. They had a spirit body. Yet it's not a physical body. I asked the angel about the bodies that I was seeing. The angel reminded me and says, "You're seeing their soul. Their soul is very real. That decision-making part of them and you is here. Your body is dead. But as you can see, feel and think you are very much alive".

The angel continues, "On the day of the rapture, at the very moment of the rapture, you're going to get your body back." There will be instant resurrections of believer's bodies. "Then you and all the other Christians will have a physical body again."

Then my mind jumped in "it's a body 2.0 its going to be better, stronger, faster." I said to myself "like the Six million dollar man"

The angel told me "When you receive the resurrected body, it will be amazing." Then a bright light spoke to me, it was the presence of the Holy Spirit. This time, this light of the Holy Spirit spoke to me.

"Your resurrected body will not tire."
"It will not need sleep."
"It will eat real food"

"It will be able to move upwards."
"I thought wow!
I asked, "You mean I can fly?"
The Holy Spirit, bright light answered "yes"

Now the Holy Spirit brought to my mind "That we will have a body like Jesus' Body. Jesus was able to appear on one side of the lake then appear 30 miles away, the next moment. His resurrected body went though solid walls and locked doors as well. This was one of the coolest ways to travel. What was it? It was the coolest mode of travel: The Speed of Thought. This is not merely our thoughts traveling, but with our thoughts we travel with our touchable, hardware, resurrected body. The entire person will move at the speed of thought. I don't know if there will be limits on this speed of thought transportation. That was going to be VERY cool. That's the ability to fly and instantly transport like on Star Trek. In this case we won't need a transporter.

I believed it all. I had no doubt. I had only solid knowing that this was all truth. My thoughts were instant. I remembered that the Holy Spirit brings scripture to mind when we need it. The Holy Spirit does that especially, when God wants to direct us. I remembered that the bible said, "The thoughts of a king are in the heart of the lord. God directs them whichever way he chooses." That really applies to me. My mind was laser focused. My mind was seemingly, effortlessly running at light speed.

Now that my body was dead, being apart from it was not scary.

I looked behind me and knew I had passed through the door of death. That moment of death was getting very

"Where are they now?"

small. I now thought "that's the very scary "door of death" I have thought of my whole life" Now it was becoming a small dot in my mind.

Shortly after arriving I saw my mom and my Dad. I saw my grandma. I could not wait to see the King of Kings. Jesus himself.

CHAPTER 8

"CHARLES DIES AT THE CRASH SITE"

Four people died soon at the crash site. They were Frank, Charles, Jack, and Sophia. These were nice, decent people. We will now follow Charles or Charlie as many called him. Charlie had noticed before he died that he was bleeding heavily from his leg. He was nervous, he felt like he was going to pass out. He even worried that he would die. He had said several times during his life" I don't need to "Get right with God" "Why do I need to fix things?"

For years he had even told others and himself "there was no such thing as God" Part of him was not convinced. As he lay there near the van. He had these thoughts in his head. In frustration He yelled out, loud and said, "I don't want to die, and I don't want to just stop existing." It was not a prayer just yelling to whatever there is that existed. That's what he believed happened at death. He laid there in the back of the rolled over van. His breath got faint; he felt his heart speed up and then slowing down. He thought to himself "in a few moments "I will cease to feel, think or experience anything." He was very sad and terrified at that thought.

"Where are they now?"

Charlie remained thinking while his breathing and heart stopped. He was aware that his body died. It was like being in a car when you run out of gas. The motor turns off; you loose the power steering, and brakes. The vehicle has no more function; it does not do anything you want it to do. Even though outside it was a sunny day. Charlie noticed darkness all around him. "How can this be", he wondered. "My body is dead." Yet the thinking, decision-making part of him was still alive and was functioning. In fact he was very aware of his changing environment. I saw this world clearly and was aware another invisible dimension was also now visible.

Charlie noticed the decision making part of him, his soul was moving. It was moving downward. He realized he was going underground inside of the earth. To say that was terrifying was an understatement. Slow at first, then faster. After just a seeming minute of this going down, he heard noises. He heard screaming and moaning. People crying and pleading "help us"

Terror filled his thoughts; He knew the screams for help were not coming from the others in the van. His spirit now came to a stop. He saw 15 ft tall angels. They angels were yelling He saw other spirits; they were others who had died. None were from the van. These other spirit people were in prison cells. There was hardly any light. The prison cells had no beds. They were not long enough to lie down in. He could see many, many thousands of prison cells. He was terrified as he drank in this horrible seen he was witnessing. He noticed far, far, miles and miles below was a huge glowing light. He realized it was a giant flat fire. "That's the Lake of Fire," he thought to himself.

He knew he was not hallucinating. He felt terror and had a clear mind. So many thoughts came to him. He realized even though there are seemly millions of people here we can't talk to each other. Even though people are yelling and crying, you felt total alone. The cell's only faced out ward. We were in like a 100-mile round shaped prison. It was shaped like a giant bowl. The walls of the prison were miles and miles high. Charlie guessed it was like a 20,000 story building. This was a giant round like shaped coliseum shaped prison. It had only inward facing openings. This was not a building like on the surface of the Earth. It was a pit open in the middle, the rock from the earth surrounding it.

Charlie saw other people in this seeming pit prison. Prisoners just stared at the other prison cells or at the lake of fire. We all knew we were in there yet we could never see another persons face or talk with them. The sounds of sadness, despair and rage crushed a person's soul. Yet there is nothing you can do. All the prisoners knew they would be thrown into that giant lake of fire far below in the future. Then again Charlie thought to himself; there is no hope of getting out of this place.

In his own prison cell he said, "I'm never leaving here" This was all more than Charlie could take. Yet, he realized "there is no escaping, leaving, hope, or water in Hades". You can't die because your body is already dead. The heat was so bad. He thought It must have been hundreds of degrees down here.

An angel, now demon flew by Charlie's cell. He started to ask the demon a question. As soon as the Charlie opened his mouth, the angel lunged at the prison cell. The angel said "don't you ever talk to me!!

"Where are they now?"

Charlie was filled with terror. Charlie waited a long time there. Finally the demon left. He waited and then screamed out "Is the real or in my head?"

A different demon raced over to Charlie's cell. The demon said "That's a question I always love to answer." The angel said, "We really, really hate Jesus, and really, really hate you humans. He continued, "Someday in the near future your body is going to be resurrected"." Your body and soul will be reunited here in this cell". "You will then feel more pain"." Smell more intensely this sulfur". "Then shortly after your back in your body you will stand before the King of Kings" "He will say I never knew you"." Shortly after that, you and the other prisoners will be thrown into the lake of fire" "Millions and millions of angels will be down in the pit with y'all"

"Your resurrected body won't be able to die." With that Charlie continued to cry, shake and grind his teeth. He was beginning to feel deep hatred. He wasn't even in Hell yet. This was Hades, the holding cells for Hell's future inhabitants. Charlie remembered learning as a kid that the earth was 7,916 miles straight though. That was going in a straight line from one side to the other. Of that, 7916 miles, mankind had only mined or explored less than 1 tenth of 1 percent. This 40 mile deep pit was seemingly in the center of our Earth. This giant pit of Hades was like less than ½ of one percent of the volume of the Earth. Most people alive on the surface of Earth had never seen or knew this place existed. Charles was devastatingly aware that he would never be back on the surface of the Earth again.

CHAPTER 9

"BACK ABOVE GROUND, ON THE HILL"

The van had rolled sideways and end over end to the bottom of a hill. One passenger, Alice had never lost consciousness. She sat thinking in the rolled over van. She remembered herself bouncing around as the big van spun and flipped down the hill. She later would tell her friends "this must be what it feels like when an amusement park ride goes bad"

The spinning made her sick just to think about. She had even thrown up twice at the crash site.

Remarkably she had no bleeding. It felt like her left hand was broke. Her left shoulder was out of socket. Her left hip and foot hurt badly.

"I'm alive," she thought. Then she remembered, what had just happened. She could see a few things from the back seat. She had seen the big van drive towards and then drive over a couple of the old boards. She had yelled, warning Frank about the boards. Yet, it all happened in just a few seconds. Before the accident no one had heard or was able to process her warning.

"Where are they now?"

She soon realized she was the only person awake and moving. That was a little scary since there were 14 passengers in that van.

There were a few unconscious friends outside the van. They did not look good.

Alice took a deep breath. She was a Christian, so she thought "God what should I do? I need your wisdom." In her mind, she got a few answers rather quickly. "Check on the others, get help. Don't give up or give in to fear."

She also felt the admonition of "Don't get side tracked." Okay she said to her self "those are kind of odd answers."

She started thinking about her unconscious friends and co-workers strewn around her. She started to fixate on each of them. Then she began to worry about them. "What if everyone is dead"? She felt sadness, and the tears started. It was taking hold of her. It had taken only a few minutes to realize "I'm doing it, or should I say not doing the right thing." She said to her self "I am not doing the things God told me to do"

She white knuckled it. She forced herself to stand up. She then wiped her tearing eyes. She hobbled over to a corner of the van. She pushed her hurting, dislocated shoulder on a corner of the van. It took a moment, but success! She got her shoulder popped back into socket. "Wow that hurt" she screamed as no one was listening.

"I bet a nice long softball bat would make a good cane." She said to her self. "It's much better than nothing." Her foot was killing her. She searched the debris. After a couple of minutes of looking, crawling and stumbling she found it. "Aha, you'll do nicely," she said to the new long softball bat. She grabbed it, leaned on it and stood up. "Relief" she said.

Okay she was encouraged now. She searched a minute for her purse. Back at the cemetery, she had put her cell phone in her purse. She found the purse and her cell phone. She tried calling and texting, still nothing. She slid the phone in her pocket. There was no reception. "95% charged," she said. "I'll need it."

She started hobbling around the crash site. She was checking the others. At the moment none of them responded to her. "Are you okay? She asked, while gently patting their head and hands. She started putting her hands on their wrists and necks. She was feeling for a pulse. "Whew" most of them had pulses. They were banged up and bleeding. But most of them were alive.

"He makes 10" she said 10 counting herself with those who had pulses. She figured the other 4 might be dead. She smiled hoping maybe I'm just not feeling for their pulse correctly. "I'm not a Doctor." She said, "maybe they are okay." Frank was in the presence of the Lord and loved ones. Charlie was very alone in pure agony.

She prayed again "What should I do?" The answer did not present itself quickly. She could not climb up the hill to flag down a car. "Oh no" she said no one will know we went off the road. We didn't show any signs we went down the hill. No broken guardrail. "We missed it," she said.

Seemingly there were no witnesses. Then she remembered that there are many custom homes in the middle of the giant Geiger Grade Mountain side. She remembered there was a maze of dirt roads on the side of the steep mountain. "If I find a dirt road," she said, "maybe I can find someone's home."

"Where are they now?"

Alice turned her head looking for a dirt road. At first all she saw were sagebrush and rocks. She could see the beautiful valley and Mount Rose far away. Looking again she saw a thin line. "Aha, there you are." She said as you noticed the dirt road. It was maybe a mile away.

She walked down to the road and walked again about a mile until she saw a house. She was excited to see a home. It was an old home that was big and kept up. She walked to the front door of the home. She knocked; a minute later an old man came to the door.

"We don't get people come up to our doors way up here." The old man said. "I bet not," Alice said. "Are you okay?" the old man asked. "You look like you've been thrown down the mountain." The old man laughing asked. "We were in an accident and our van went off the road." "We" Asked the old man. "Yes, our van is back up the road a little way. Everyone is injured or dead. Can I use your phone? My cell phone has not had a signal for long time." "Sure come on in", yelled the old man. She hobbled quickly to the house phone and called 911.

While she started the call the old man walked to the refrigerator. He pulled out iced tea and cheese. He poured two glasses of tea. He cut up a few slices of sharp cheese. He then cut up a couple of apples. Lastly, he poured a box of crackers into a small bowl. He quietly placed snacks next to where Alice was sitting. She was now talking with the dispatch. Alice whispered "thank you" to the old man. Alice was on the phone with 911. Several managers started listening in on the call.

Alice yells, "We went off the road. Dispatch says "Slow down mam, I need your name and location." My name is Alice Belzar. Alice whispered loudly to the old man "What's your address?" "7773 Dry Gulch Lane", the old man answered. Dispatch "is the accident at that location?" Alice answered "its about two miles away." "Our van went off Geiger Grade road. We tumbled and rolled down the hill."

"There are a lot of us. I'm the only one conscious at the moment" Dispatch, "how many people are in the van?" "There are 14 people counting myself", answered Alice. Alice continued, "We went off the road maybe 10 minutes after leaving the cemetery.

Someone in the dispatch background was overheard saying, "Y'all might be going back up to the cemetery."

Dispatch; "how fast were you going?" "I don't know maybe 35", said Alice. A different person at dispatch says we have a general idea where the roll over may have happened. Alice hearing that replies; "we had just seen Mt. Rose the second time." Dispatch; "what do you mean a second time?" Alice: "we'll as you drive down the hill you come around two corners. At one curve you see a glimpse of Mt. Rose. At a second curve you see Mt. Rose for a longer time." Dispatch replies "okay, that's helpful, anything else?" Alice; "yah, we had just drove by a big billboard sign." Dispatch; "do you remember what the sign said?" "Yes, it was at the second Bucket of Blood salon sign.

In the dispatch background someone shouts "I know where that is" Alice replies; "good, are you going to send help now?" Dispatch; "Yes, responders are in route now." Dispatch background; "Should we go to the crash site or where Alice is?" Alice overhearing says; 'Why don't you

"Where are they now?"

come to where I am. There is a dirt road here and then you can drive over to where my friends are." Dispatch replies; "perfect, we are also already sending deputies to the main road and sending a search and rescue helicopter. Medical is in route as well."

"Please hurry, some of them are in bad shape', replied Alice.

While Alice was still on the call with dispatch a huge, longhaired Maine Coon cat came close to her. Whenever Alice grew frustrated or sad, the big cat would move closer. It moved just close enough to pet. She did not pet it. The cat a couple of times also gently tapped Alice's arm.

Dispatch; "We want you to stay on the phone until they arrive."

Alice replied, "I need to go back to the site." Dispatch pushed back and restated; "please wait where you are at?"

The old man chimed in; "I have a satellite phone it reaches all over this mountain." Dispatch says; try calling me now. If the call comes thru, and holds then you can slowly go back to the crash site." The old man called the dispatch from the satellite phone. Dispatch; "okay that works, and we have a strong signal. Go ahead and go back to the crash site. Keep the satellite phone with you and turned on." "I will and thank you," replied Alice.

Alice grabs the snacks and tea. The old man quickly grabs several couch pillows. She hobbles over to the old man's 50-year-old International truck. They throw in the pillows and climb in. They zip over to the crash site. Alice is now on the phone. The old man is driving. She continues to confirm that they still have a phone signal. "It's perfect," says Alice. "Yep" replies dispatch.

The old man drives the first mile on the dirt road quickly. "It's still like a mile over there," says Alice. "We are going to have to walk the rest of the way", says Alice. "That's not necessary," says the old man. "This old truck can get there easy. We can drive there even if there is not a road." With that said, the old man drove the last mile easily. He had no problem. He did negotiate a few rough spots and through hundreds of sage and rabbit brush. They got close up to the van. Alice quickly hobbled out, and over to four people. The same four people, that earlier had not had a pulse. She walked over to Frank. She felt his neck. He still had no pulse. She gently cried as she looked at him. She noticed he had a slight smile on his face. The old man gently said, "He's dead". Alice walked over to Charlie. She checked for a pulse. There was no pulse. "He's dead," said the old man.

Alice got to the last of the four. She checked Jack again. "He's got a weak pulse", she said. "Good" said the old man. She then checked Sophie. "She's got a pulse to", said Alice. "Good, good" replied the old man.

CHAPTER 10

"JACK AND SOPHIA LEAVE THIS LIFE."

Alice checked on the other nine passengers. They all had a pulse. Two of which had a weak pulse. That was Jack and Sophie. Alice tries rousing them. Sophie is a friend of Alice. Alice pats Sophie's hand several times. "Wake up, wake up Sophie", Alice repeats. After a few attempts at this, Sophie does regain consciousness. Alice breaks into a tearful smile. "Your back" whispers Alice. "I thought we lost you." Sophie states, "It's okay" Alice grabs Sophie's hand. Sophie says "Something can't be lost if you know where it is. If I am absent here, I'm with Christ. I mean with him side be side." "I know I know said Alice. You and I have prayed for years at hard times. I know you're like me you even pray for little things and God answers those prayers. God likes to show us he's even happy to give us small things. I still even pray for good parking spaces. That I find the parking meter that still has time left on it from someone else. God answers those things. I'm so happy he answered my big prayer to keep you alive." Alice was holding Sophie, "I love you Sophie" "I love you too replied Sophie". No one could be a better friend than you," replied Sophie.

Sophie continued, "I'm doing good" I'm surrounded by the Holy Spirit." Alice says, "I believe it." Sophie continues, "I think this is what happens to Christian's when they die. When a Christian lives trying to stay connected to God, they often sense his presence. When Christians have his spirit, that is the Holy Spirit living in us, He never leaves us."

Sophie continued, earlier I was surrounded by the Holy Spirit and angels. I could still also see you, but I could not respond to you. I am just now able to speak." "I feel like the apostle Paul, I want to stay here. I also want to depart and be with the Lord." Alice say's "I don't want to say goodbye". Happily though, Alice was relived that Sophie was ready to die. Being around a dieing person not ready to pass is very hard. Unnerving, it is very heart breaking. Today, in most hospitals those dying are sedated to spare them and the surrounding living persons the anxiety of experiencing death and dying.

Sophie was holding Alice's hand. Sophie began singing a song called "Your Glory" by the Planet Shakers. Sophie began to notice less of her physical surrounding and more of the warmth of the Holy Spirit. She again began seeing more and more angels as well. She slowly noticed that she had disconnected from her body. She tried to tell Alice it had happened. Alice could not hear her. Sophie was immediately in the presence of the Lord. Scriptures immediately flooded Sophie's mind about Christ love for her. She instantly knew this was a happy time as well for God. "Precious in the eyes of the lord is the death of one of his saints." God was very glad to have his believing child home. Sophie also was reminded and knew in a moment that God deeply loved and even very much liked her.

Sophie could see Jesus standing directly in front of her. Her mind instantly recalled scriptures stating how great God's love for us is. She knew he also specifically loved her. Jesus loved us so much that he died to save us. She could see the scars on his wrist from the crucifixion. He did that so we could be with him. Now, she was face to face with this God who loved her. It was overwhelming, to see the Creator of the universe. This was the same God who had created her inside her mother's womb. She knew she was home now. This was where she wanted to be.

Sophie could see her body behind her. Alice was calling her name. It quickly dawned on Alice that Sophie was no longer in her body. Alice smiled and cried as she sat staring at Sophie's face. Alice thought about what she must have be experiencing now. Sophie thought Alice would be blown away to see the risen Lord now. Sophie was feeling fantastic. She felt a little sad for Alice. She instantly knew Alice would be good. In fact she also knew she would see Alice again. Sophie struggles to say, "Au revour."

Sophie began seeing other people and more angels. The other believers did not have bodies like on earth. But she could tell they were people. Jesus was still walking beside her. His body was a touchable body. At one point Jesus had patted her hand. She could feel the touch of his hand she did not have her resurrected body yet. She felt like she had not traveled at all to be in Christ's presence. She felt as though she was in the same space as she was in. Just in a separate dimension. Literally in an invisible dimension, simultaneously here on the Earth.

She began seeing some of her saved family members. She saw her grandma, a great ant. She could hear beautiful music. She went a little further with Jesus. The very best part of being in heaven is the fellowship with the Lord. Then, neither Christ nor Sophie could be seen. They were very close to Earth. Maybe even in the same space as Earth. They were just out of sight.

Alice looked down and notices that Sophie does not have a pulse. She tries rousing her again. She tries several times. Unlike before, this time she does not wake up. She wonders if Sophie has died. The old man and the cat walk over. Alice asks the old man, "Do you think she is dead?" The old man says "yes." The cat lies down on Sophie's hand. Alice is overwhelmed with missing Sophie. They had been good friends for several years. She leans down to hug Sophie. As she is hugging her she hears "Au revoir." she thinks Sophie said it but her lips never moved. She tries waking Sophie again, but there is no response, nothing.

Suddenly the old man yells to Alice. "Alice please come over here." Alice turns to see where the old man is. The old man is knelling next to Jack. Jack is writhing around. Please don't let me die he says. Alice hobbles quickly to Jacks side. Jack is moaning and yelling again. He is chanting "don't let me die, don't let me die. I'm in Hell. I'm in Hell."

Alice and the old man compassionately try reassuring Jack. Jack partially opened his eyes and said, "You don't understand I'm in Hell." Alice knows that Jack is exactly where he says he is. She knows that Jack is not a Christian. Jack is seeing life without the source of all things good. He's in a place he's never been. A place of literally nothing that is good. Everything good is no longer supplied or available.

"Where are they now?"

She say's "Jack your need to believe on Jesus and you will be saved." "It's too late; all this Jesus saving a person can't be real. Jesus is dead and gone. I'm going to be dead soon any moment. Jesus can't help me he's dead." With that Jack grimaced and passed out. Jack did not wake back up. Alice checked for his pulse. Now he did not have a pulse. Alice turned to the old man; almost on cue the old man said "I'm sorry Jack is dead."

When Jack had grimaced he could tell his body had stopped working. He was aware that his body was dead. He was starting to freak out about the fact that he could still think. He, like Charlie believed that when you're dead that's it. That nothing else happens after your body dies. He believed there would be no consciousness, no thinking. So far Jack was experiencing and learning that was not the case. Jack even tried to go back in to his body. Now that he was dead he could not control his body.

Jack thought back to a time when he had seen a small-injured bunny. He tried to help the little bunny but it was just scared and would have nothing to do with Jack. At the time Jack thought that the bunny could do nothing to save its self. Jack realized that was how he was now. Now that he was dead. He no longer could change any events in the afterlife. He was filled with terror, knowing he no longer had control of his life. In his case he could not control anything in this new to him afterlife.

Charlie had heard his heart beating before his died. He actually heard it stop. That alone was horrific. As with Charlie, Jack knew it was sunny outside where he had died. As Jack's body died, he saw and even felt darkness around him. It felt like he was in a separate dimension, while still in this dimension. He kept thinking "at any moment now I will cease to be able to think or experience human feelings."

The core of a person, as some theologians call the decision making part of a person, was very much alive. He was aware that he was going inside of the earth. Since he did not have a touchable body, he moved easily. He picked up speed as he went down deeper and deeper into the Earth. He began to hear screaming, some screaming was very sad, some screaming was extremely angry. He himself was feeling very scared and extremely angry. "This can't be happening. I don't believe in this garbage." He quickly remembered back when Frank told him "believing in something or not believing in something does not make something real."

Quickly Jack thought "I exist and I'm like a ghost now. I'm alive but I don't have a physical body. Terror filled his mind, he didn't know what to expect but so far it was bad. Anxiety was growing in him.

He traveled through rock and dirt. The claustrophobia was more than he could take. The phobia couldn't kill him. He was already dead. After first slowly and then faster he arrived above a large pit. It took a moment to grasp the size of this pit. When he was alive he had seen several 100-story buildings above ground. This pit was like hundreds of times taller. In this case deeper. This pit is like 100 miles around.

He hovered a few moments over this nearly unbelievable sized pit. He was lowered slowly along the sides of the pit. He now could see spirit people inside of the walls of the pit. "This thing is like a prison," He thought.

"Where are they now?"

He noticed something else he had never believed in. Angels. They were huge, like 15 feet tall. More fear filled his mind. It now hit him more. "This place is so hot, it smells very stale and like sulfur,"

CHAPTER 11

"SEARCH AND RESCUE"

While Alice was sitting with Jack she hears a noise. The old man and the cat also turn to look to where the sound is coming from. It's coming from the sky. It's a helicopter. For the next hour plus, several helicopters arrive. Many sheriff deputies, EMT vehicles and techs also arrive. They are all intent on getting the four dead and nine living victims to treatment. Alice and the old man are helping as much as they can. Alice is hobbling around to each of the crash victims. There were 14 van riders including her, four of which were now dead. The nine others were injured. Alice was the only injured person up, awake and functional. A medic quickly comes over to Alice and Jack. The medic accesses Alice is stable and quickly checks Jack. Alice says Jack was conscious a few minutes ago. The medic checks Jack's vitals. Two other medic, run over to Jack. They work on him for twenty minutes. After that one of the three medics announce Jack's time of death. Alice says "no I think he is alive, I have been praying for him and I keep thinking I see a sign he is breathing." The medics agree, but they add

"Where are they now?"

he is not breathing, he has no heart beat. We have not seen any signs of life for the last 20 minutes. A separate 4th person, a doctor comes and examines Jack. He says this man is absolutely dead.

Frank, Charlie, and Sophie's bodies were taken to local funeral homes.

CHAPTER 12

"BACK TO THE LAND OF THE LIVING"

Frank's body is taken to a local mortuary. It's been six hours since he died on the hill. It's close to five hours since he was pronounced dead at the scene. His co-workers bodies, of Charlie and Sophie were also in the same refrigeration room.

In Heaven Frank has been visiting with his mom and dad. They both had died six and two years before Frank had died. Frank was enjoying this warm time of catch up. It was great to visit with his parents again. Both of his parents were very friendly and glad to spend time with Frank. Everyone who approached Frank was beyond words friendly.

In Heaven Frank was also visiting with a hospice care Chaplin who he had become good friends with during his dad's passing. He was enjoying that and a time with his grandmother. His Grandmother had died close to 30 years previous. His Grandmother Alice had raised him the first 4 years of his life. She had sold Frank and Ann their first home in 1990. She had encouraged Frank to study the bible after he became a Christian. She herself had started

"Where are they now?"

churches. She and her little sister lived hard. They had built a house with their dad. Alice's dad even lowered Alice and her sister on rope to dig out a well. Frank's grandmother was a renaissance woman.

During all these warm reunion conversations, Frank's mom paused. Franks mom looked at Jesus who was standing very nearby. Jesus nodded and then Lou, Frank's mom nodded back. Lou said softly, "Frank you're going back". A little uneasy Frank asked "going back where?" A grown man came up and said "it's all right dad you will be back." Frank instantly knew who the man was. 38 years earlier when Frank and Karen were together she had got pregnant. He had wanted at that time to keep the baby. At the time Karen said no way. Without Frank's agreement she had an abortion. Frank knew he was meeting his then aborted son for the very first time.

With no answer given Frank began feeling his connection with his old body again. He thought it can't be. He said. "There's no way I'm going back, back to my body. Especially, since I have been here for so long." Frank figured he had been in Heaven for seemingly weeks. Slowly Frank began feeling pain and soon woke up back in his body. "Oh no, not all nonsense this again……"

CHAPTER 13

"HE LIVES, JACK COMES BACK FROM THE PIT"

Jack is experiencing the horrors of Hell's jail of Hades. While lying in his cell he notices little dots of lights arriving down into the jail cells. Then afterwards he sees the silhouette of a person in those cramped jail cells. He could not see or count all the souls arriving into the huge Hades jail. He figured there had probably been thousands just in the brief time he had paid attention. Even though the souls were visible as human, like he, they had no regular body. Something else that was awful is everyone is naked in Sheol. Believe me there is nothing arousing about it. It's just shame we all felt. I did notice no silhouette looked like a child.

Every once in awhile one lone tiny light would go upwards. I asked a less cranky angel, "What is the small light going upward mean?" The angel replied. "That's when someone's body is resuscitated. That is the person's spirit returning to their body. Usually they quickly come back. It's fun for us when a light returns here. Sometimes it takes a while."

"Where are they now?"

As was my new normal, I was cowered, curled up in the corner of my cell. There was not enough room to stretch out. I was weeping, crying, and grinding my teeth, feeling enraged at God I was feeling like an insignificant dot. I was one of billions of souls in this pit, the prison of Sheol.

While my soul laid there lamenting in anguish. My completely lifeless body was being loaded up into an ambulance.

The three bus techs or as they call it when they carry a dead person was a meat wagon, were not in a hurry. My body looked very rough. I was cold and white as a ghost. The three medics had seen many like this before. The man and the women upfront drivers were not fazed by my lifeless body. The third female medic, who was to ride in the back with me, stared at me. She asked the other two medics. "What do you think this guy is doing now? The other two medics did not hear her. She looked at me and closed my dead open eyes, she was thinking about her own mortality. She hoped this stranger was in better place. Again she asked the other two medics. "What do you think this guy is doing at this very moment? They both nervously replied "nothing" The other women added. "It's kind of like what "hot lips" said on the show Mash, you live; you die. The guy medic then added, "That's the end, zero, zip nada. He is biologically dead. Every one of his systems has stopped functioning. He is not experiencing anything."

Part of her accepted that and part of her did not. She thought "I don't want to stop existing when I die." That was a terrifying thought, an even worse reality if true.

They finished loading up my body and slowly drove back on the dirt road. The ambulance was moving slowly on the few miles of bumpy dirt road to get back to the main Virginia City highway. The tech in the back seat named Betty was looking for a cell phone signal. After she got one she started texting her friend about what they might do after she got off work. It was a nice relaxing time. After 15 more minutes of driving they got on to the freeway. It was common practice when a passenger has been pronounced dead, to go at a safe speed of travel. No lights or sirens were necessary. I had been pronounced dead a couple of hours earlier.

Jack's soul himself was miserable. It took all the strength I had to stand up. The spirit body in Sheol has so little energy. On the earth surface Jack's body was 6ft 2inches. My current spirit body was seemingly the same height. So when I stood up I noticed I could not stand up all the way. The cells were a little over 5 feet tall.

The heat in Sheol was so hot. Jack asked an angel who was more reasonable than the others how hot it was. The angel replied "it's something over 300 degrees up here. Dozens of miles downward, below, towards the fire it's more like thousands of degrees." Jack was stunned. The angel gleefully also volunteered, "Yah there are even more demons down the lower a prisoner is placed. A soul even gets more maggots and larger worms in their cell. You must not have read in the bible that maggots are under you and your worm is on top of you. I always love telling the new arrivals about the maggots and worms. Have fun I got to go group scare". With that the angel flew downward to a different cell. Jack looked down at the now arriving several maggots at his feet. Being naked and barefoot was now even more awful. Again there was nothing he could do. His mind never left the state

"Where are they now?"

of being in terror, anger, despair, sadness. He was feeling rage.

Back on the surface, Betty asked can we take our lunch break now. The driver said "let me call in to dispatch," he called dispatch and dispatch said "your clear for a 30 minute lunch." With that the bus backed in to a national fast food Mexican restaurant parking space. Betty took everyone's order. She sent it on her phone and waited until they brought the hot spicy food out to the ambulance. As the three sat there eating a lunch, Jacks soul was overwhelmed as usual. In Sheol you never get a mental break. Jack was no exception. A very unfriendly couple of demons came over in front of Jack's cell to scare Jack. He lay there staring at the angels while they made fun of him. They even plunged their hands in towards the back of the small cell. Jack was maybe an inch past the grasp of the powerful ancient beasts. The stench of maggots was right under his nose. He tried to not think about the smell. He slowly imagined the spicy smell of Mexican food. He loved that while on the Earth's surface. For the first time since his arrival in this Hell of Sheol he thought about God. He thought, not even spoke "God thank for the good things I enjoyed when I was alive."

Suddenly a demon "screamed what are you doing" at Jack. Jack looked weakly at the demons at the front of his cell bars. The demons were now enraged. Grasping at Jack, they were screaming "no". Jack noticed he was turning into a small dot of light. He felt himself as a small dot of light going back upward. He moved quickly upward. An angel was screaming "we will be waiting for you. The screaming subsided and seemed farther away now. Jack was traveling upward faster now.

Back in the ambulance the three techs were enjoying their lunch. Jack had been pronounced dead a few hours earlier. The guy glanced at Jack who was still white. Bob the male tech glanced over at Jack. Bob had just taken the finishing bite of his spicy burrito. He looked at Jack again and thought "Did I just see his finger twitch?"

"Hay you two I might have seen the stiff's finger move" Betty said no way. That guy Jack bled out at the scene. The other lady grabbed a stethoscope and checked for a pulse. There was not one. Now all three techs were staring at the body. Bob asked, "What is this guy's name again." Betty replied "It's Jack. Betty put the stethoscope back on Jack's chest. Bob and the other female tech held both of Jack's hands. Bob started saying "Jack if you can hear me squeeze my hand. Betty started praying for Jack. Bob and the other lady started squeezing and shaking Jacks hand.

Jack who had been dead for hours was still moving towards his body. His soul going upward finally stopped. He weakly squeezed Bob's hand.

Startled, Bob looked down and murmured "He just squeezed my hand" Jack the dead guy, asked Betty. "Yah I don't think he is dead anymore," replied Bob. The three techs started trying to rouse Jack. Betty checked again for a pulse. "I got a pulse, it's weak but it's there."

Jack was now hearing the three techs. He even heard them, loud and clear, yet he could not respond to them. He also was in terror about where he had been for the last several as he thought days. He was more afraid of going back there than replying to the techs. He tried hard to speak. His human body now was weak and unresponsive. He started to remember the accident, and highlights from his life. He

"Where are they now?"

remembered he had bled a lot. He remembered he had died on the mountain. Alice was holding his hand when he died. With great effort Jack murmured "don't let me die". Then one of the three techs said, I think he just moved his lips. He said that again, this time they heard him. "I'm alive, I was in Hell" they heard him rhythmically repeating. He started to open his eyes, and then his body failed again. Jack knew his soul was going downward just like the fallen angels had said it would. There was nothing he could do. He fell for a minute or two and then came into view of the pit. The prison looked as awful as before. While Jack was descending he could see the same demons near his cell. He heard them laughing and joking that he was coming back. He heard a demon say they never learn. Another demon laughed and another demon said shut up stupid. Jack thought learn, learn what? Jack weakly asked "Jesus please, have mercy on me" He had never thought or said those words in his life.

Now again he felt his soul stop falling and it started going towards the earth's surface.

The three techs were frantically trying to resuscitate Jack. After a few minutes, they started slowing their attempts. Nothing was working. Unknown to them Jack was quickly rising to reunite with his body. Jack arrived back in his body. Again Jack's hand twitched. Betty who had been holding his hand felt his fingers move. Jack opened his eyes. He stared blankly at the three techs surrounding him.

Bob asked "Jack can you hear us? Jack struggled to answer. He whispered yes. The techs, gave him two litters of blood. Jack was in a lot of pain. He was very glad to be back among the living. Jack blurted out "I accept Jesus that he died and was buried and rose again." To the techs it was more like a whisper. Jack repeated it, this time loud enough to hear. Bob and the other med tech just stared at Jack. Bob said "please sir just calm down. The other nurse nodded to Jack in agreement. Betty, thinking she should acknowledge what Jack had said. Betty replied, "Jack I'm glad you accepted Jesus. Betty did not know what that meant, but felt good to validate what was important to Jack. Jack smiled. The three med techs got into their seats and got the ambulance started. They started calling dispatch saying we got a live one. This time the bus started driving fast. Jack thought to himself, thank you Lord for bringing me back to above the ground. Thank you Lord for not having me go back to that prison, that place of torment. Jack now had a feeling that he was not alone anymore. Jack had never talked to God before. Now he could tell God was real. God seemed to be in the presence of Jack. More accurately, Jack was now aware that he was in God's presence. That presence is a warm, wonderful feeling for a forgiven person. That's a terrifying presence for the unforgiven person. Jack just laid in the back of the ambulance as it roared down the freeway to the hospital. He was not really able or willing to converse with the techs. He was just glad to be back. This new feeling that he was in God's presence was better than anything he had experienced in his life. He knew he never wanted to leave that experience.

The ambulance got to the hospital and several nurses and a doctor quickly examined Jack. He had lost a lot of blood. He was still alive but they needed to stop the now restarted bleeding. A doctor said. "I don't know how this guy is alive. But we will work to keep him that way. Take him to surgery" with that an unconscious but alive Jack was wheeled to surgery.

CHAPTER 14

FRANK'S BODY

Frank's body was picked up at the roll over site. He was taken to a local mortuary. To get to the mortuary, the bus drivers, drive up to a gate. At the cemetery gate the groundkeeper lets you in. Today Sam and John were at the gate. They asked if they could ride on the bumper of the ambulance. Bob said "that's fine; we are just dropping off one man. So they all rode the almost quarter mile from the gate to the mortuary.

It is a well groomed cemetery. They drove though the narrow gothic section. The three bus and two grounds keepers just stared at the old impressive mausoleums and huge head stones. Many had ornate wrought iron, giant head stones; some even had huge marble angels. Those people, all had levels of respect; even a little fear and wonder as they drove slowly throw the narrow Goth section. Some of them wondered what the dead people were doing now and they wondered what they themselves would be doing when they were dead.

They rolled up to the mortuary and unloaded Frank. They rolled him into the building. Frank was then toe tagged and put in a refrigerated room.

At that moment Frank's soul was in Heaven. In addition to being with Christ, he with his parents, grandmother and now son, Out of left field, Frank's mom had said "you have to go back." Frank said no, Frank said I didn't even get to into the city of Heaven. Frank's dad said you'll be back before you know it. Frank started to feel cold. Earth is colder than ever, said Frank. With that Frank's mom and dad looked and smiled at Frank. He smiled back. He was glad he had not gone back into his body. Frank felt himself drift off to sleep. He had not thought there was napping needed in Heaven. He started to wake up and again he felt very cold. He also felt like he was physically connected to something. He felt like he was chained, like he had a boat anchor attached to him. He was not sure what it was or what to think. His spirit body felt very tired. He suddenly realized he was in his fleshly body again. Frank struggled to open his eyes and that was a challenge. He realized he was in a large sleeping bag. He could barely think or for that matter move. He struggled just to find the strength to move his arms. He slowly moved his right arm up to the top of the inside of the bag he thought was a sleeping bag. He even thought "why am in a sleeping bag?" Frank was able to get a single finger out of the sleeping bag and slowly struggle to pull down the zipper. Frank was trying to figure out why he was so weak. Why was he in this dream, he had been moments ago in Heaven. He remembered that his mom and dad had said he would have to go back. "Oh no I'm back in my Body. He did not know why he was back.

"*Where are they now?*"

Being back in his body seemed like a nightmare. He started to remember about his kids, his wife. He pets. They were all precious to him. But he did not want to be back in his body. He very much wanted to be in Heaven instead. He felt cheated that he never got to go into the city. In Heaven he had mostly walked with his parents a few friends and Jesus in beautiful giant fields of flowers. It was surrounded by mountains. Animals were peacefully grazing and playing around them as well. He left that beautiful place to show up back inside of a bag. He realized he was in a body bag and not a sleeping bag. He was less than thrilled to be back in his now very weak, pain filled body.

He got one hand out and struggled to open the bag so he could look out of it. He could see he was alone. He could see several other bags with bodies in them. He realized "wow, I am in the morgue." It was cold in there and Frank was still barely able to move. Frank was in a giant refrigerated cold body storage room. Also know by its nickname "the cooler."

The overhead lights had been left on in the body storage walk in cooler. Sam and John were getting ready to go home up for the day. They were going to go get a couple of beers. Sam said, "Hay man we got to go turn off the light in the storage room."

Frank was now struggling to sit up; he had one arm out of his body bag. He struggled slowly, he got his other arm out and was working to sit up on the table he was on. He was so weak he passed out. He came to again, and was struggling to sit up when Sam and John walked in. At this point Frank was gray and a mess to look at. Sam and John saw Frank struggling. They heard of stiffs waking up, they had never seen it happen. Sam yelled "Oh my God, that guy is alive," John ran over, to the nearly, sitting upright Frank. John yelled "quick call 911" Frank had just his two hands and the top of his head out of the body bag.

The bus or ambulance had been gone for maybe an hour from the mortuary. Dispatch called the ambulance and said "you got to go back to the cooler at the mortuary." "Sure, why" asked the med techs. "Just get over there a sap. I'll let you hear the call from the mortuary. The bus turned around and started quickly driving to the mortuary. The dispatcher replayed the 911 call from the meat locker. Sam talking loudly said, "Hay the guy named Frank is not dead he woke up and is struggling to sit up. Come help this guy we don't know what to do." The dispatcher connected the ambulance driver to Sam on the phone. Betty in the bus said "we hear what happened." Sam was okay buy nervous. "Hay Sam we are driving fast back over to the cooler. Stay calm and is Frank okay and calm? Sam replied "he's lying back down but he's mumbling, so he is alive." That's good he is resting, sorry about the scare he was pronounced dead hours ago. So this is a surprise. But this does happen, it's very, very rare but it happens. Our eta is 5 minutes." They got there and Frank was smiling and mumbling incoherently. The transferred him from the cooler slab to their gurney. They quickly got him to the hospital. He needed immediate surgery to close up both of his femoral arteries.

CHAPTER 15

"FRANK AND JACK START SHARING."

Frank and Jack are both now at a local area hospital. There are five hospitals in the Reno-Sparks metro area. For the moment they both were recovering in the same hospital. Neither knew the other was there. They both took a day to rouse. They both now were expected to live. Knowing how long it would take to recover was not known.

Frank was now sleeping in his hospital bed. A nurse came in to check his vitals. As she was in there his IV low fluid level alarm started beeping. Frank woke up as the nurse was silencing the device. Now awake, Frank sat in the dark a few minutes. A local tv reporter asked if he could visit Frank. You can go in for one minute. I need to be with you as you talk to him. They both walked from the nurses, station to Frank's room. Hello I'm from the channel 5 news. I would like to set up a time later to interview you about the accident. Yes, only if you also ask me about what happened when to me while I was dead for a few hours. Frank answered. Sure, I'd be happy to record that as well. The reporter left and Frank began remembering his time with

God. Frank begins asking nurses and doctors who lived and died. Can I see them all, did other passengers die as well as me? A nurse says "a man named Jack died. But he resuscitated a while after he was pronounced dead. Wow! Where is Jack now?" The nurse said let me check. She left the room and went to the nurse's station. A few minutes later she came back in the room. "He's here in this hospital; he is two floors up in room 805. He is in the physic ward. He has been talking of a being in a giant prison. The prison is supposedly Hades." The nurse continued, He's been ranting on about angels, and fire. He says he had no body but he was himself. He says he was really there."

"Can I see him?" Frank asked. The nurse paused, "I don't think you want to see him now. Let his sedative kick in." Frank was less than thrilled to talk to a maybe sedate Jack about his Hell experience. Frank knew he was not calling the shots on Jack's care. The nurse then asked "I can check if it's okay to see him. Would you like that? Frank relied. "Yes". The nurse said, "I'll see what his and your doctor says". Frank thought and he wanted to hear about more of Jack's experience. He also knew he could help Jack.

While Frank sat there staring out the window. He thought, "I need to see the rest of my softball team." He thought of his own experience. He thought about what he had heard of Jack's experience. He wanted Jack to have experiences like his own close time with Christ and past family members. Instead Jack got what he thought he wanted, freedom away from God. That would be Hellish. Frank knew the best part of going to Heaven someday again was going to be a face to face relationship with Jesus Christ

"Where are they now?"

the Lord God. The wonderful fellowship with other Christians, the having a touchable resurrected body, the City of Heaven itself. Imagine being able to move, at the speed of thought. Those things pale in comparison, to being with the lover of your soul; as well as spending time with the being who really loves you as well.

Frank was lost in his own thoughts when his wife walked in. There was a kiss and hug. They spent a long time going over how they were both doing. They were both talkers. At this moment they both had a lot to say. Frank was almost talking over his wife Ann. His wife would listen a while and then give the look. This look said, really you not going to give me a chance to talk. Frank picked up on that and let Ann speak. This exciting give and take conversation went on for almost 90 minutes. It was like the Bible says in Proverbs 27:17 it calls this type of speech "Iron sharpening Iron". Both Frank and his wife Ann enjoyed catching up. It had only been a little over two days since the accident. But it was an action packed two day period.

Ann was blown away that Frank was pronounced dead at the crash site. Then hours later he awakens in a refrigerated holding room at a local mortuary. Frank's relationship with Christ has just gone through the valley of the shadow of death. Frank told his wife "Christ was there as it promises in the Bible." To Frank his relationship with God was not just one sided. It was not merely something he believed. It was reciprocal on God's part. Frank continued, "God is really, literally waiting for us at our death. It was like when you fly to another city and upon arrival. Your friend or loved one is there waiting at the gate for your arrival. This was something I don't want to ever forget." Frank continued "I know

I have to tell others about this wonderful, warm, and fulfilling relationship connection with God.

He and his wife were still enjoying their conversation. The nurse came back and said "Both your and Jack's doctor approved your visiting with Jack. Both doctors think it may be good for Jack. In fact Jack asked his own doctor if he could talk to you."

Frank and his wife both did a head nod to each other. "Thank you" Frank said to the nurse. "When should I go see him?" "He is showering and then eating lunch. So maybe wait an hour" answered the nurse. "That sounds good", answered Frank.

The nurse left the room then Frank and Ann decided to eat lunch together in Frank's room.

CHAPTER 16

"FRANK AND JACK CATCH UP".

Frank and Ann sat, ate and visited for another hour. Ann said "I'm going to go. I will come back later tonight with the girls. They want to see you." "Good, I want to see them", Frank replied. "Good luck talking with Jack. He sounds altered. Don't let him rub off on you" "I won't." Frank replied. "Oh and be easy on him and not too pushy" Frank knew the pushy remark was in regard to him sharing his faith with others. "I'll be kind." Frank replied. Ann replied, "Alright then, see you tonight, bye." With that Ann kissed Frank and left the room.

Frank knew he vacillated between two extremes. With some friends and family he usually did not talk constantly about his faith in Christ. He had found after 37 years many people recoil from the mention of Christ. Most people are willing and even interested in talking about God. But when you bring up the name of Jesus, your listener tends to get uncomfortable. On the other side is the truth that sometimes the person you are talking to is very interested in Jesus. The thing to do then is to ask them if they would like to have their own relationship with Christ. Frank realized he had become a little reluctant to strike up a conversation with others about Christ. Frank had the fear of rejection. He also was reluctant to "Close the deal, or make the sale." He would usually just talk about Christianity and Christ. Not leading the willingly interested person to the foot of the cross. Frank knew he had to talk about being born of the spirit. Not just saying God's in my life, but also to say I want Christ to be in your life as well. Frank was reminded internally that he had to pray for God's wisdom. Frank needed to seek God's will for dealing with things. Frank did not always know the right course of action. He needed to lean on God for understanding. Not just white knuckle though tuff decisions himself.

All of these thoughts went through Franks mind. He thought, I want to talk with Jack. I want to comfort Jack. I'm ready to listen to Jack and offer words of wisdom and comfort. Frank did not know it yet, but Jack was very interested in talking about his going to Hell/Hades trip. Jack wanted to make sure he never went there again.

Frank walked from his room to the elevator and went up to Jacks room. He was nervous and excited to talk with Jack. He would find out soon Jack was also excited and a little nervous to visit with Frank.

Frank was walking stiffly and now in a little pain. Just walking from his room to the elevator was almost too much for Frank. He walked in to Jack's room. When Frank came in Jack's room he had a pained look on his face. Jack was sitting up in bed looking forward to seeing Frank. He mistook Frank's grimaced look as reluctance. Jack felt Frank probably did not want to be in there. Frank said "good morning

"Where are they now?"

Jack" Jack miss read Frank again. He felt Frank was being too formal and even a little cold. "Morning" replied Jack. "Is now a bad time? We can visit another time. You seem less than happy to be here." Frank looked up; he was a little surprised by Jack's statement. "No, no this is a perfect time. I'm just sore from walking. I was seemingly fine when I left my room. Just walking down the hall to the elevator caused a lot of pain. Walking down the short hall on this floor is even more painful. I realize I'm not quite the stud I thought I was. This accident has done a number on me. But I do look forward to us visiting. At the moment I just need a chair. Or I might collapse on to the floor.

Jack was relieved and now concerned for Frank. "Please have a seat." Frank hobbled to the lone chair in the room. "Ah", said Frank. So tell me about how you are doing? "Well, Jack started; I want to share about my accident experience. I also have a bunch of questions. I also want to hear about your accident experience". "Go ahead, I'm interested. I also have no real estate appointments today." Replied Frank, they both chuckled.

"Well I had a rather rough experience after the accident. It was scary as you may remember. We were all in good moods, just relaxing. You were driving and it seemed like in about 10 seconds things changed. Something happened and then the van pulled hard to the edge of the mountain. We quickly went over the edge. It seemed like a movie. We started to tumble and I was quickly knocked out. After just a few minutes, I woke up. It was quite. Like too quite. I think I was in shock. I was just staring around and trying to figure out what had just happened. I felt very tired and weak. After being awake a few minutes, I fell back asleep or passed out.

After several more minutes I saw Alice get up. She struggled and started walking away from the Van. I tried to call out to her but my voice had no sound. I felt nervous and worried that I was not doing okay. I could barely move and I was bleeding from several spots. Becoming frantic I was able to get myself to an upright position. I was starting to worry that I may not live, I became angry and scarred." Then I blacked out another time. Jack looked up to see if Frank was listening. He was. "It sounds awful, I'm sorry you had to go thru that." Frank said. "That's not even the bad part." blurted Jack. "Okay, go on" said Frank.

After a long time I heard Alice talking she was talking to someone else. Then her voice was louder and louder. Until I could tell she was near me. I could not even talk or open my eyes. Then I felt her touch my shoulder and then firmly held my wrist. She was seemingly doing that to check my pulse. That freaked me out. Did she think I was dead? Part of me did think maybe I was dead. I could not reply to her. I could not speak. I could not open my eyes. But I was thinking. The fact that I was thinking made me decide I was still alive.

At that point I didn't know what to do. I was not in charge of my body anymore. I couldn't make it get up. Alice started trying to rouse me. She was shaking my shoulders. Some other voice I did not recognize said "here let me try this." So I began feeling moisture hitting my face. I slowly opened my eyes to see an old man flicking water in my face. Alice yelled "he's awake." Alice started holding my hand and asking me if I was okay. I just kind of starred at her. She began to tear up a little. "Are you okay? She continued to ask." I tried speaking again and I could. "I don't think so."

"Where are they now?"

"What do you mean?" She asked, with a concerned look on her face. I barely was able to whisper "I think I'm dying. I don't know what to do."

Alice looked even more concerned. Then I blurted out "I'm not ready to die." I remember I said that over and over again. Alice said "if you're going to die. You can have some peace as you die." "Frank, I knew she was going to say that God crap you have told me about." Frank wide eyed, just continued to listen. "I whispered louder to Alice. It's too late for me. You know I don't believe in this Jesus stuff. It's too late. With that I felt my body stop working. It was like if you ever drove a car and then ran out of gas. All of the sudden you can't steer. You cannot brake. All the accessories stop working. The AC and radio turn off. That's how I felt. My body was not responding to any of my demands. I could not talk, I could not move. I could tell my body was disconnected from the part of me that made decisions. I had this insight that I was dead. There was no time to process this new reality. The creepy thing was that I could still feel emotions and think. That actually bothered me that I was still alert. I had just figured when you die that's it. No feeling, no thoughts, nothing.

I quickly realized that's not my reality. Within a few moments I felt my essence or soul going down ward. I somehow knew I was going into the actual earth. You know like down into the dirt. I was moving through rock. I knew I was going deeper into the actual dirt of the earth. Slow at first and then faster and faster. It took a few minutes. As I was descending, I was filled with terror. My mind was filled with paranoia. As I got near the end of my descent I heard screams of terror. I realized I was not alone. My spirit stopped descending at the top of this giant pit. I just hovered over this pit. It was really much, much wider and many times deeper than the Grand Canyon." Frank interrupted, "How big was this pit." Jack replied, "Well it was miles and miles deep. I have seen some valleys that are like 30 miles across. This pit was like 100 miles around. It was almost unfathomable how big this pit was. It was larger than any structure or valley I had ever seen in my life." What do you mean structure?" asked Frank. A little annoyed Jack answered, "I mean it was not like looking down from a tall mountain. From some tall mountains you can see for many miles. You can see many mountain peaks and the mountain peaks between them. This was like a stone building that was bigger than these giant valley view's I had seen on earth. Frank just sat there listening even more intently. Jack continued. Frank you need to listen to me. This was a prison, or maybe a jail. I say jail because I had a feeling this was temporary. Some angel told me while I was there, "This is not even Hell, that's coming in the near future." I could see what must have been millions or probably billions of little rock prison cells in the side of the walls of this giant jail or prison pit.

After I observed this spectacle for a few minutes I floated myself into one of these prison cells. This cell was so small. It was not much larger than my body on earth is. Jack realized that he had said something a little odd. Feeling a little self-conscious Jack looked over at Frank. Frank was just relaxing and quietly listening.

"You don't seem moved or shocked by this story I'm telling you. Do you think I'm making it up Frank, asked Jack. Frank was not unfamiliar with Jack's grumpy, annoyed side. He also knew information that Jack probably did not know. Now leaning forward Frank started to talk. "Did you know in the United Stated alone there are over 63,000 ER physicians? There are over 56,000 surgeons, there are over 35,000 cardiologists." "So, why are you telling me those statistics?"

Jack interrupted. Frank calmly stated. "SO many of these doctors have had patients die. I mean die while they were in the presence of the doctor. Many doctors have had patients that come back to life after they died. They had a near death experience. Not all patients talk about what they experience but some do. Of the patients that do talk, more describe about experiences similar to yours. Many of the NDE survivors will not even talk about what they have experienced or seen on the other side.

More of the NDE people talk of scary stuff, than of the peaceful stuff. That's something to be concerned about. Many doctors think it's much more than half. Most experts think that is because many NDE patients don't choose to talk about their experience. In fact so many people who approach death and die are drugged to keep them from being anxious about their own death. There are millions of Americans each year who die and they are mentally "out of it." Who knows what they have experienced. Did you know according to the Ourworldindata.org website over 60 million people die a year? That's with the world's current population of over 8 billion people. Jack stared at Frank kind of blandly. Jack asked how and why do you know any of that? Frank replied, I was in my own way wanting to validate you. I also wanted to empathize with you. The things you are beginning to describe are very heavy. They are heavy for a reason. The reason it is heavy is because you experienced the truth.

I came to the sobering conclusion many years ago that someday I would die. I want to be at peace when I die. I do not want to fear what's coming next. I became a Christian 37 years ago. It came about because of a relationship gone wrong. My heart was broke at the time. It was not to cheat death, but I felt unloved and realized God loved me. I realized love is stronger than steel. It's even stronger than death. God's love for all of us is actually real. So is his repulsion of sin. I realized to have God's acceptance I had to deal with my own sin and guilt. Jack started to interrupt, Frank continued, "Hold your next thought. I had to deal with my sin and guilt GOD's way. God is literally running the enter universe and that includes what happens to little life forms like us. He oversees everything before, during and after our life. Jack I believe you because many, many other people have had a near death experience. And the majority of them are scary and terrifying like yours.

Jack sat there looking a little irritated and stunned. "I don't know what to do now." Jack started, "This experience I had was real. My body was dead for couple of hours. I was in another place it was not a dream. It was real. I can still remember so many details of being there. The smell was awe full. The pit must was larger than anything I had ever seen on Earth. I asked one angel or I guess they are now demons, how deep is this pit? He said it is 20,000 levels deep. I quickly calculated that to be like 40 miles deep. The demon said "it's something like that. I also had never seen a valley as huge as this pit was. I asked this less irritated demon. "What is this like 50 miles around this giant pit? No

"Where are they now?"

he said "it's more like over 100 miles around. This pit can handle billions of you people. You're just a nothing, a no one down here." With that the demon left me alone. Frank I felt terror and so alone. Even though there are all these other people there, you cannot talk with them or interact with them. I knew I would never leave. I knew there was no way out. I knew that I had caused myself to go there. I also knew God had allowed me to go there. All hope is gone there. The cell is not even large enough to lie down in. I was sad and mad. I despaired even of my own existence. Believe me nothing is worse than being in Hades. No lost love, no health problem. No lost romance. Maybe a spouse leaving you or your own child dying is close. I had an experience of both as a younger man. That pain was incredible. Being in Sheol felt so despairing, I had now felt those feelings of loss and then all my new terrible feelings of loss and despair. It was worst than I can even describe. The knowing it was never ending, that had I chose separation from God made me hate myself. I felt so much hate.

Frank added, I have learned that God does not want any of his people and their souls he made in his image to go through what you went through.

God not only calls us his friends but he wants an intimate Friendship relationship with us. He also calls us his bride. Then Jack asked, why did I go through this and you didn't? Frank answered; I was a mess before I came to Christ. In some ways I'm still a mess. It has taken me years to learn things that I needed to learn. Jack, I still have and feel the pull of sin in my mind. As a Christian you have two natures in you. I still want to please myself and be wrapped up in myself. But when you are born of the Spirit, meaning now God lives along side of you. God the Holy Spirit puts his desires in your heart to please him. God gives you the desires of your heart. He puts new wants and desires in your heart or mind. Every person who has the Holy Spirit living along side of them now has to wrestle with doing God's will and doing their own will. That's a lifelong battle. Many times your old desires and your new God given desires pull in opposite directions.

With that Frank and Jack just sat quietly looking out of the hospital window. They where processing all that they had both heard and said. It was more Iron sharpening Iron going on.

CHAPTER 17

"THE FLASH BACK"

The next morning Jack decides to go see Frank again. He's now more interested in this God stuff. Jack sees several nurses and doctors running around. He hears on the hospital intercom "code red to room 733." He knows that is Frank's room. Jack rolls quickly to Frank's room and sees people working franticly on Frank. Jack fears the worst for Frank. Jack hears a doctor pronounce the time of death. Jack feels bad for Frank. He even feels bad for himself. He wanted to talk more with Frank. Now he did not know what to do.

As Frank died this 2nd time he again entered to the deeper presence of God. This time as he passed he could see three bright lights. They were the persons of the Godhead. They began speaking;

"We knew all of mankind before they were born. We knew each person before they were created." Now one bright light spoke. "I knit you together in your mother's womb. With precision I made you, all of mankind. I made a universe with order. Everything worked together perfectly and it was very good."

Now, three bright lights spoke, "we are complete, the three of us, are God. Separately, we are one God." "We made man to be with us."

Now Jesus as bright as the sun spoke. "I made and hold all things together. All matter would expand apart except for my power. I hold it all together for you and of my own good pleasure. Someday I'll let it all go. I will then create a new Heaven and new Earth."

Jesus continued, "I made you in our image. Now the three bright lights spoke, "Mankind has the ability to feel, think and love." "We gave all of mankind dominion over the Earth." "Humans have the ability to choose"

"You can choose to live close with us. Meaning you can walk side by side with us. Or you can be at a distance and ignore your God."

"We knew all of mankind would drift away and each would follow after their own way. We made a way for you to return to fellowship with us. Your sin had hid our face from you. But to those who believe on Jesus and in the power of his name we forgive. Our spirit will then live in and with those believers."

"As God we know the deepest longing of your heart. In fact we put it there. The greatest desire of all mankind is steadfast love. We made you so that nothing in your life would satisfy your heart more than our love. The love of a spouse or friend can be warm and wonderful. Our love for all men far surpasses even that. We love you, and we like you. That truth will be felt completely when you pass though to us at your death."

"The person that has the Holy Spirit living inside them, That's one of us living in fellowship with you." The single light continued. "I will come into your heart and mind, if you desire me to. If you want nothing to do with me, I will stay away."

The three bright lights continued to speak. "The love we have for you is deep and warm. This love IS us, we ARE love, and we are not just only loving. We are love itself. "We stay inside your mind, if you want us to come in, we will. If like many people you want to keep us out, then we will hold back. "If you accept us, then you will know us. If you say "no thank you" you will not know us. You will not see us at your death. Many shun us during their life.

"We have no pleasure in the death of those who reject us. But, to the one whose sins are forgiven and accept our gift of pardon. That person's death is precious to us.

CHAPTER 18

"FRANKS BACK"

While Frank was still with God, Jesus says "Its time to go back". "No pleads Frank. I do not want to go back to the cold world. No one really thinks much about me or loves me. No one there, except my three daughters and wife care. Frank was feeling sorry for himself. Once again Frank's son in Heaven had words of encouragement for his dad. Dad remember Jesus, I do replied a irritated Frank. No, remember that Jesus knew you and was thinking of you. He thought of everyone while he was going to and hanging on the cross. He thought about all the future souls who would accept his payment. Jesus never took his mind off of all mankind. That means Jesus was thinking also about you. In his mind Frank could see Jesus staring at him while he was going to and hanging on the cross. Frank felt on fire with Love as he could see Jesus staring at him over 2,000 years ago. Jesus does sustain and think of all of us, all the time. No one is like the Lord. Everyone is precious to the Lord. The Holy Spirit then said, "Go be with your family, be a witness for Christ. Tell others about Christ. I love you.

I'll bring you back here soon. There is a lot more here that you have not seen."

"Like what? Frank asked. With that question, Frank woke up again in his body with a janitor looking at him. "What do you mean, like what? I thought you were dead," asked the janitor. Frank and the janitor just looked at each other for a moment or two. Both of them thought "what's up with you? What's your deal?" After more uncomfortable staring, Frank said "never mind".

The custodian ran to go get a nurse. He had not been with a person after a near death experience. Not at the very moment when that person comes back to life, in the land of the living.

Frank felt called "a fresh" even invigorated to be a soul winner. I wanted to tell others about my conversion story. I felt conviction that God was compelling me to give his testimony. I was convinced that being passive in telling others about my conversion story was sin. "I know It was not pleasing to God to be a "secret Christian." In a minute, two nurses' came into my room. "Well hello, Mr. Locksley" they said "I understand this is your second time back to the land of living." They waited to see what my response was. They were not sure what my mental state would be. I said I'm doing good and feeling good. A doctor came in to check me. The doctor was busy checking my heart, breathing, reflexes etc. The doctor said "Take it easy Mr. Locksley. You're not exactly stable. But we will keep an eye on you." "Thanks Doc," I said. I felt like I was back for good now. I had a mission to tell others about Christ. I figured God would let me live a while to do that.

CHAPTER 19

"MAKE AN ETERNAL DIFFERENCE."

Frank and Jack both were released after several days in the hospital. They both felt compelled to share their testimonies. It was as natural as breathing to them now, to talk about their near death experiences. They told any friends and family they saw about their NDE. They both would tell waitresses, convenience store clerks. It was getting bad, they would talk too much to total strangers. It's like the Bible says "they could not help but speak of the things they had seen and done," Act 4:20. Many poor strangers did not have time for in depth conversations. They both knew it was bad when one day Frank and Jack where talking non-stop to a couple of Home Depot employees. Frank was on a different Isle than Jack. They could hear some Christian conversation coming from the other isle. Frank stopped talking at the nice Home Depot electrician and went around the corner to see who was talking about Jesus's crucifixion. It was Jack holding a poor paint employee verbally hostage.

"Where are they now?"

Now that Frank and Jack were both annoying their families and friends with constant talk of Jesus they both volunteered to become volunteer chaplains. They spent many training classes with a chaplain. To be a licensed chaplain it usually requires a degree. There was a shortage of licensed chaplains so trained volunteers where being allowed to help. They could help when the need was more than a professional chaplain could manage by them self. Frank and Jack both got police scanners. They both got an app on their phone to monitor some emergency 911 conversations.

Frank and Jack knew the end could come for either of them, at any time. They also knew that anyone and everyone is on the conveyor belt of life. You really don't do not know when your time of death may come. You need to be ready for it and help those who may not be ready, get ready for their own death. One day in their volunteer chaplain training the teacher told them a couple of key things. "When you're at a scene and a person is going to die, think of your own role as being like a coach. A coach has players do what they don't want to do to get the players to where the players where they want to be. If you're near death person is talking about not being ready to die and asking what do they need to do. Tell them about the Gospel. Do it in a calm, friendly, respectful even loving way. Be sincerely gentle. They will quite probably accept Christ. If they don't continue to be calm, friendly and respectful. If they don't want Christ or get angry, stay with them until help arrives or they pass. This phase is not easy, but it is important to the person approaching their own death. The teacher said I've had many people convert as they feel their own death getting closer.

"That's gold" said Jack. "It is" agreed Frank. Also Jesus said the world will hate you. Expect the world to be against you because get ready for it, IT IS. Stay calm and don't show signs it bothers you. The person may bash or make little of your Christian world view. Believe it or not it's normal now to be made fun of or even hated for believing that Jesus is the ONLY way, truth and the life. Remember Jesus's words, "the world will hate you for my sake, be of good cheer, because I have defeated the world."

Head nods came from both Frank and Jack. As they both left class Jack said do you think we have to have that negative mindset. Frank asked "what negative mindset." "That the world hates us", replied Jack. Well, yes but don't be negative about it. Stay upbeat as you usually are. Just when you talk about your conversion story or the bible or Jesus don't let it bother you if people make fun of you. It's a biblical input on it's not personal it's just business. The person had a problem with God before you even talked to them about God. We should not add to any negative image they may have. Let's just speak about Jesus positively to non-believers. Hay do you want "In & Out" burgers for lunch, asked Frank. "Let's do it replied Jack. After lunch I need to get ready for a talk at the Church.

CHAPTER 20

"FRANK'S MESSAGE AT A CHURCH"

Frank has been a Christian for 37 years. He went to a Bible college. He and Ann his wife had taught Sunday school. Frank had taught a men's bible study for over a year. He also taught creation science to adults at the same church. I say all this because, now years later Frank starts and stops church attendance. He believes the same things as he did. He believes them even more deeply. Yet, he no longer teaches other Christians. He realizes it's once again time to speak more about his faith and his own conversion. He remembered God is really not pleased with us being secret Christians. Frank was convicted that he was not flying the Jesus flag high enough. He did not talk about Christ to others enough, but when he did many times they give him "the look". That look you get when you talk to a non-Christian and they look at you like you're crazy or giving them poison. Even talking about Christ is not the same as showing people Christ. It would be like talking about how wonderful your spouse is, constantly and then never showing that same person your spouse. That is the big challenge to show the non-believer that Jesus is currently alive. That he is very active. Jesus is even thinking about you at this very instant. That's important to impart to non-believers and for believers to be constantly reminded of.

Frank had started Bible College 38 years previous. Frank did not graduate from Bible College. Frank knew many people who knew him may not even know that he was a Christian. "I've got to tell people about how God is working in my life. They may then see how often and when God is working in their own lives. God is working constantly on us individually. At a molecular level it's every second. The Bible says he holds all things together. That's a continuous action, never stopping.

Frank was not involved with a church congregation. He had attended a local church a few times. Sunday was the following day. On that Sunday morning Frank and Ann were lazily sitting and watching the CBS Sunday Morning show. Out of the blue Frank said. "I'll go talk to the pastor and see if I can give my testimony." Frank's wife replied, "They probably won't let you talk to the congregation since they don't really know you." Frank sadly said "you're probably right. A few minutes later a commercial for the local news came on. Frank did not watch the news. Some of it was good. So much of it was political. Frank murmured "TV is so much social engineering. His wife just shook her head. Frank sat there like a deflated bump on a log. During the local news commercial, the TV ad mentioned an upcoming story. "Coming up at noon we will have part one of the Frank Locksley story. As some of you know he was pronounced dead. Then several hours later he woke up in one of our local mortuaries. You

"Where are they now?"

don't want to miss this story. Now back to the CBS Sunday Morning Show."

Frank was all the sudden excited and shocked. He did not even know his story was going to be aired. "Wow, that's very cool" said Ann. "I only talked for a few minutes to that reporter while I was in the hospital. I bet it will portray me as an ignorant Christian." Frank said. With that Ann walked out of the room. Frank walked out to his back yard and sat on an old bench swing. He sat there frustrated and encouraged. He felt an urge to cling to the encouragement and ignore the frustration. "Are you telling me to be encouraged God? There was no answer. But Frank started daydreaming about what he should do with this small bit of public exposure. "So Lord, how do I go from talking about you, to getting non-believers to believe? Lord non-believers and many Christians have forgotten this one simple life changing truth. Jesus you are the prize. It's not only avoiding Hell. The most important thing to non-believers and believers is to have steadfast love. You Christ are the only being who offers that love, your love is eternal and you deliver it.

I felt very close to the Lord again. When I pray and thank God. When we talk to him about the kind, generous things he has done. The Bible says he is there. He inhabits the praises of his people. I could sense that the Holy Spirit was there with me, just like the Holy Spirit had been with me when I died.

"Lord you are here with me now." I could feel the presence of the Lord around me. It was just as when I had died, but this time I was still alive. Ann looked out the back window, to see if I was okay. "He's fine, she told her family. I was sincerely in the presence of the King of Kings and Lord of Lords. From the French doors, to Ann, I looked like I was holding still, sitting motionless on a swing. My daughter asked her mom, Is Daddy okay? Ann said I think so. He's out there talking to someone. He's probably on his phone. They both walked away from the French door's, back to the kitchen. They both saw my cell phone on the kitchen table. They both shrugged their shoulders, and went into the living room.

I had felt the presence of the lord many times in my life. "This is what Heaven is; it's literally being in your presence. If I were much closer I would experience the scripture stating; No man can see the Father and live. God can handle all the intimacy with us. We on the other hand cannot handle all the intimacy with God that's available. I know I, like other Christians look away. We take our mind off of fixating on the splendor of God. I like other Christians have been in that close spiritual connection with the Holy Spirit, only to look away at some point. During that connection the world's becomes the last thing on my mind. The world real allure tugs on my heart yet it is quieted. As soon as I start focusing away from the Holy Spirit, the other desires of my heart start grasping for my attention. The sad thing is I do this willingly. I chose to take my eyes off of the Lord.

So I had all this going on in my mind. Meanwhile my wife and kids keep looking at me. I'm in an old bench swing in my back yard. They periodically glance at me from the windows. I know I have to "come back in" The main attraction of Heaven is you have a continual connection with Christ. Once you have that connection, everything else is less important on your priority or interest list.

"*Where are they now?*"

I got off the swing and went back in the house. My wife and three daughters were busy. My wife asked if I was okay. I said "I'm Fine. ' I thought to myself "I was actually like a mountain climber coming back down from the top of Mt. Everest. Even like the feeling of the first kiss with someone you love. But I can't stay in that mode. I had to function here on Earth. I needed to be a normal person, a husband and a dad. I was literally lost with my head in the clouds. In my case I was enraptured in being in the presence of The King of King's." I felt I had to operate normally again. So I started on my regular routine. "I'm going to go ahead and start cooking some bacon, hash browns and sweet breakfast sausage." It was therapeutic for me to cook. I was mindful and focused on cooking and I was also mindful of where I had just been. I had been in the presence and in fellowship with the King of Kings. Though I had not traveled physically anywhere, I was there.

I finished cooking breakfast. We all nibbled on the food. I tend to over cook the bacon. Some of the five us sat at the table, some eat on the couch watching TV. After everyone ate, I sat at the kitchen table relaxing. I also reluctantly looked at the state of the kitchen. It was as usual a greasy cluttered mess. I shook my head, smiled and got up to clean up the kitchen disaster.

I spent the next 90 minutes doing dishes. I cleaned counters, took out the garbage, then the recycling. As most of you know these are common activities, especially for a Sunday morning.

I decided to go to church that morning. I really did not know anyone in the church. I had not gotten involved with other individuals. I would go and listen to the sermon, sing and enjoy the worship songs and leave. I never did any of the extra stuff. I rationalized because my wife and kids were not attending either. I would feel guilty going to church and then felt guilty when I returned. I would still get something positive from going.

That Sunday as usual I parked and was walking through the outside quad area. There was coffee and doughnuts'. About a third of the church goers stand out there before service and socialize. It's a nice time to fellowship with other believers. Since I don't have anyone I know there I usually kind of sneak thru them to get inside the church sanctuary. This same Sunday a couple of members who I did not know stopped me. "Hey we saw you on TV this morning. I had no idea you had died." Another guy said yah then he went to Heaven and then hours later he came back to life in a body bag at the morgue." Well actually I came back in my body in the storage refrigerator at the local mortuary at Mt. View Cemetery, I replied. Now dozens of people were staring, listening to me. I felt flattered, nervous and like I was grandstanding. I just stood quiet for a few seconds. Some worship music started and one guy who sensed I was uncomfortable said, "Hey folks let's go inside the sanctuary". I was relieved. The little crowd started going inside. I went towards the back as I usually did. This time several strangers sat around me. A few worship songs played, each time they started to sing the congregation would stand. When the congregation stood and sang. I noticed people were turning to look at me. The TV appearance was bringing me some unwanted attention. During the sermon many times people were turning around to look at me. Even the pastor was randomly looking at me.

"Where are they now?"

After the service the pastor went to the back of the sanctuary as usual to visit with exiting people. This time as I was trying to quietly leave the pastor approached me.

"Hay Frank," the pastor said "wait up. Let's talk about your experience. Do you have a time we can get together?" Sure" I replied. "Good I'll call you later to set up a time" replied the pastor. I got into my van, kind of surprised and flattered by the attention I had got from the church congregation. Many were watching and looking at me as I backed out of my parking spot and drove off. I did wave and smile a little as I drove off. It was less than a ten minute drive home from the church. As I was pulling up to my house my cell phone rang. It was from an unlisted contact. I thought maybe it's the pastor. I answered and sure enough it was the pastor. "Hay Frank can you share your death experience next weekend." "Do you mean with you or with the congregation? Both actually, I want to hear more and the church should hear about your experience" replied the pastor. We'll I need a little more time to prepare. Can I do it say in two or three weeks? Also I think Jack should give his going to Hades and coming back experience, I replied. "Who is Jack" asked the pastor. "He's a co-worker, friend and now Christian who recently accepted Christ. Jack's testimony is very compelling," I replied. "Sure", answered the pastor: "do you have his phone number and I'll give him a call" "great yah, I'll send you his contact now, I replied.

I now sat there in front of my house and sent Jack's contact to pastor Jim. I walked back in to my house. My wife asked "how was church?" I had not been there for a while. "It was good, apparently many people saw the teaser on TV earlier this morning. Several people were staring at me. At the service people sat closer to me than normal. Usually I just go to the back and am alone. This time I sat in the same area, and then people got up from where they were sitting and moved to the back of the room. The pastor apparently even knows my name now. He stopped me after the service. He asked if I could share my life after death experience. I said yes and that church ought to have Jack share his experience as well. The pastor said sure, so the pastor is going to give Jack a call and then have both of us talk about our experience. Isn't that cool I asked? Ann replied "well there is your wish to talk to people about your experience and conversion. I thought he would be reluctant to let you speak at the church. I guess I was wrong." It was a logical assumption, I thought the same way, I said.

I walked out the front door and sat in our porch swing. I called Jack to discuss the whole matter. Jack did not answer, when it went to voicemail I started to leave a message, and then Jack called me. I stopped recording my message and switched over to Jack's call. "Hey the pastor of your church just called me and asked if I would give my testimony of my life after death experience. He said you thought it was a good idea. Did you say that? "I did" I replied "people don't hear enough of the scary, convicting parts of scripture. Non Christians and believers usually stop listening to the scary parts of scripture. Jack your NDE (Near Death Experience) is powerful. It combined with your conversion experience will strengthen believers and truly convict non-believers that death is not the end of the road. It's not even a bend in the road. It's a shallow doorway with a paper thin door, instantly allowing the believer to be more with Christ. The unbeliever starts instantly moving away from all things that

"Where are they now?"

are good. I told the pastor all that. I said that it was important for the congregation to hear all that as well."

"Wow, that's a lot of pressure to live up to" replied Jack. "I do think I have to tell people now, about what happened to me. I fell like I'll burst if I don't tell others. It's like the apostle Peter said, we can't help but speak on those things we have seen and heard from the Lord.

Jack continued speaking of his near death experience said; I don't want anyone to go where I went. I know most dead go there. The vast majority of people never return like I did. They are down there now. Millions or perhaps billions exist in pure misery, terror, gut wrenching sadness and despair. The heat there is so bad, they have no hope. So yah I can speak on what I saw and what Jesus has done for me." I then said somberly, "Christians and non-believers will benefit from your testimony."

CHAPTER 21

SERMON DAY

I drove the short three miles to my church. On the way I was praying that I would stay calm. I also asked God for wisdom, and boldness. I asked God to use me to help bring listeners to saving faith. Even though I had written what I wanted to say, I asked God to give me the words to say. Especially if I was in front of people and froze up. The Bible says do not worry about what to say but at the right time the Holy Spirit will give you words to say. That's in Mark 13:11.

I felt overwhelmed and excited to share my salvation story and near death story. I did not expect that when I got to the church for there to be lots of cars, but there were. There were seemingly hundreds of cars. Something that kind of freaked me out was also seeing TV station vehicles there. There were maybe twelve different networks in the parking lot. There were Spanish, Mandarin, Japanese and even Hindi reporters there. Many cars were even on side streets. This church building is in a residential area. It was a good size mini campus. But the crowd there this day was larger than I had ever seen it have. It was much larger than

"Where are they now?"

the Christmas or Easter service attendance. Those two days of course are always the largest attendance most churches ever have. So now my ego and fear were climbing. If I became arrogant God would not use me. I kept the mindset of I need you God. This was nothing like I had ever done before.

I was thinking if I did this under the power of the Holy Spirit I could help many of the listeners. I also had a huge scary thought that if said a few dumb things I could screw up non-believers for their lives. I had given a copy my message to the pastor, before the message. He had said I would be fine. Many pastors run their message though some staff before they deliver a message. Since I was not a pastor I did not have that benefit. I kept silently praying that I would not freeze or destroy or distort theology. I also felt calm like the Holy Spirit would help me; As the Holy Spirit had done for thousands of years, for all of us. God gives all the words to say when we need it most. In fact the Holy Spirit will help us chose our words at the same time we need them and ask him for help. I just needed to speak slow and keep praying even while I was speaking and the Holy Spirit would give me the correct words to say.

As I got out of my car, reporters and some of the congregation quickly came up to my van. That was intimidating. I just said hello and good morning to people as they approached me. I started to get questions and statements from reporters, I just said, "I'll talk more about my experience when I get inside the church." I slowly made it over to the front door of the Church building and then made it to the pastor's office. The senior pastor opened the door and let me in. He closed the door behind me.

The pastor said "hay good morning, Frank are you ready for this mad house? I have not seen this many people here ever since I started preaching here. I said I think I am as ready as I can be. The pastor had me sit in the front row. That was where he, his wife and guest speakers sat before a message. I was nervous and excited. A couple of people got up and read the announcements. Then the pastor got up and told an opening joke. I really paid light attention to what he was saying. I just wanted to get through my material and not chicken out. In my mind I was praying still that God would help me speak the words I needed to say. I checked out enough to where when the pastor introduced me. I did not react. His wife nudged my shoe and I snapped to attention. I stood up and heard some applause. I thought I have not even said anything. I walked stone-faced over to the podium. I had the Holy Spirit empowering me, making me feel like I could speak. I also had a smaller separate feeling and thought that I should somehow stop speaking. This was a big and scary thing I was about to do. I took a deep breath then started speaking.

"I know many of you don't know me. I preached 37 years ago to a small church, then only twice after that. I had felt so nervous and unprepared to deliver a sermon. I still feel a little like that. I'm going to tell you a little about my life before I was born again. Then I'll speak on my death or as it's now called a near death experience. I was born again in 1986. My life went sideways after I fell in love with a girl. I made the mistake of making her the center of my life. She disappointed as anyone would when put in that position. I didn't see a reason to continue living. So I cried out to God to take my life. I said if you turn my life around I will live for you. God came into my heart. I had never experienced feeling God's Holy Spirit presence in my life. The reason I'm up here today is because I'm convicted about people and their souls. Something that breaks my heart is how many people don't seem like Christians. I feel so many parallel's as to how George Whitfield and Jonathan Edward's felt. Some of you may know who they were. Some of you may not. Whitfield preached in fields because local churches did not like his animated style. Back then clergy wrote and then read the sermon to the congregation. He memorized his sermon and spoke passionately. Jonathan Edwards preached the famous sermon "sinners in the hand of an angry God." He was a Hell fire and brimstone preacher. Edwards spoke that sermon in 1741. Something that may offend some; is many denominations and their churches are what is called seeker friendly. Teaching only what is politically correct. They have chosen to not teach on Hell, and Death. Many churches don't even talk about being saved. It's taught and then presumed that everyone makes it Heaven. There is no accountability and no need of Christ's work on the cross.

Feeling guilty can be destructive, yet properly handling your own conviction concerning your own sin is life changing. Many listening non-Christians and born again believers as well, do not want to be convicted over their own sin. Jonathan Edwards said non-believers are just dangling over Hell. It is merely God's good pleasure, an act of his will that keeps them from dropping down into Hell. I agree with Jonathan Edwards. Now I'll put on my theology hat. No one is in Hell at this moment. After the rapture, then the 2nd coming of Christ, then the literal, physical 1,000 year of reign of Christ, then after that there will be the "Great

White Throne Judgment". After that judgment, Lucifer and all the other rebellious angels and non-believers will be thrown alive into Hell. Currently as of this moment, Hell is empty. But a different terrible place called Sheol in Hebrew or its called Hades in the Greek is very full. Sadly, though it also has room for many, many more. The Bible says it's a real place. The Bible says its hidden deep in the Earth. Now for just a little science and geology here, in 1970 the Russians dug a small 9 inch diameter hole. The hole was completed in 1992. It was and still is the deepest penetration on Earth. It went down 7.6 miles. The Earth is 7,907 to 7,926 miles if you could travel thru the center of it. Mankind has not explored even one 100th of one percent of the inside of the Earth. The word in Hebrew is Sheol or in the Greek, Hades, it surely can be hidden deep in the Earth and we would never know it. The Bible says it's there. Hades is currently many, many miles under this surface of the very earth we are currently on.

Currently studies of NDE or Near Death Experiences are very fascinating. This has been studied thoroughly for many decades. Currently in modern cultures where there has been reporting, it's reported between 10 and 20 % of those who are very ill, have a NDE. In countries with more advanced medication the reporting is harder to report. More and more people are now drugged at the point of their own death, that's to help with pain or anxiety of dying. It's also to help the dyeing person's family to cope with their loved ones death.

Among those who are lucid, more NDE's speak of a terrifying or Hellish experience. Those terrifying visits go more unreported; the reports of Heavenly visions get more reporting. For whatever reasons the person having a NDE (Near death experience) and the person recording the story tend to be more dismissive of the terrifying NDE accounts. Reporters and publishers are very excited to publish the beautiful, loving NDE accounts.

Today two of us are going to speak on own NDE. One of us had the real heavenly experience and the other of us had a terrifying experience. I went to Heaven and it was beyond wonderful. As much as I love my family, friends and pets, I wanted to stay there. I did not want to come back. I'm very happy to see my living family and be back with them. I also look forward to a time when I return and go further into Heaven. Now Jack on the other hand had a going to Sheol experience. Going to Sheol or Hades is horrendously terrifying. Jack then walked over to Frank's microphone. Jack mentioned "I will speak and answer questions after Frank speaks." A congregation member asked him "were you in Hell", Jack replied No, I was in what I call the holding area for Hell. That is called Sheol in Hebrew or Hades in the Greek. As awful as Hades was, it was not Hell. Hell according to the Bible receives the rebellious angels and unbelievers after the great white throne judgment. But I'll talk about my experience and answer more questions when I get up to speak. With that Jack waved and sat back down.

Frank started speaking; people ask me if our van roll over accident was life changing. It truly was. It also deepened my relationship with friends and family. It cemented my view on the afterlife. 37 years ago God placed the Holy Spirit next to me. I say next to me because he is along side of all saved persons. We are in his midst. Some like to say the Holy Spirit lives in us. I say when we are born again, He's right beside me. Like a loved one holding my hand.

When I sin, the fellowship with God, the Holy Spirit is not felt. When I "confess my sins he faithful and just to cleanse us of all unrighteousness". Then fellowship with the Holy Spirit is restored. When I live for an audience of one, meaning to love others as myself and put God first in my life. As Eric Little would say, "I feel his pleasure". Even separate from his pleasure I and other born of the spirit people, we additionally feel his presence. That is something that is not felt before "you believe in your heart and publically confess that Jesus is Lord". That statement is from Romans 10:9.

For the last 37 plus years I have felt the Lord with me. The day of the accident I felt him as I picked up the soft ball team members. I felt God close as we drove to a soft ball game in Carson City. I felt him close as we drove on Frank Town road in Washoe Valley. As we drove on that same road we saw several deer. It's on the edge of the forest that eventually reaches Lake Tahoe.

Later that day we won the softball game. We then drove to a great steakhouse. On the way to Old Reds 395 steak house everyone was in a good mood. That happy atmosphere made me thankful for having an enjoyable time. Later the group of us all wobbled out of the restaurant to the van and loaded up. We drove approximately 15 miles to Virginia City. The ride there is though the old town of Gold Hill with 150 year old buildings. Seeing the old town made me think I was glad to be alive. We soon went on the mine tour. The group leader told us several stories of miners and their deaths. That made me feel satisfied that God is there with me. Some of the others of my group were nervous to be in the mine. I was reminded by the Holy Spirit "I'm here with you." There were just so many God prompters. That's a phrase I heard in a great teaching CD series called "From the Edge of Eternity."

We had planned to see the Virginia City Cemetery. That was our last event of the day. That alone took almost an hour and a half. That cemetery was full of God prompters. The grave markers themselves, the conversations they all pointed to relationships with God. Some pointed away from God, which just made me joyous that I have been saved from the penalty of all my sins. There can be consequences from my sins. But having God place my total sins on Jesus is a peace that has no limits. I want you to know I knew I was in the presence of the Holy Spirit. I had that clarity many times during my last 37 years. The day of the accident I did as well. I had no idea I was going to die the day I died. We loaded up at the cemetery and left the cemetery. We had a leisurely 30 minutes more left of our ride home. We all had enjoyed a nice day. It was warm and sunny as we left Virginia City. There was just no reason to think in less than 10 minutes we would be in a major accident. If any of you want to skip hearing about the accident now is a good time to step out into the hall, or stretch your legs. I was the driver and the 14 of us were making small talk. I had the radio on as well. Some of us were singing along to Queen's "We are the Champions" As I was driving down from Geiger Grade road, an old construction truck wanted to pass me. I waved to the driver to go around me. As the old truck passed me I noticed he had lot of old wooden boards in the back of his pickup truck. I also noticed that they were loose. They were not strapped or tied down. Some of the boards were above the edge of the pickup bed. I remember thinking "that's not safe. If any those boards fall out it could cause an accident." As many of you know that is a winding road. Even though the speed limit is 35 some of those corners have a speed limit of 15. Well as I was coming down the hill at the speed limit I came around a corner and there it was a couple of boards in the middle of the highway. The van weighs something like 10,000 pounds. It takes longer for a larger vehicle to stop. I wanted to go around the boards but there was a big 4 x 4 pickup coming in oncoming direction. Since I was at the bend in the road and the brakes did not stop me in time, I ran over the boards. I went over the shoulder. It was surreal. The whole day had been so nice. Here I was looking at the beautiful Mt. Rose. The sun was up. It was a warm day. There was not a cloud in the sky. I thought about that all as I struggled to keep the van from going over the edge. The rollover was slow at first and then it picked up speed. I passed out at some point. One deputy later told me we had rolled down nearly 500 feet of mountain. I came to and noticed I was upside down strapped in my driver's chair. There were not any sound's, I did not hear any of my friends. I did turn my head and look behind me. All of the passengers were not moving. I tried to ask them if everyone was okay. I then realized I could not hear my own voice. I looked out the front window. I remember thinking I might not make it off this mountain alive. The most important part of my experience is this. When I came to my mind started thinking: what has just happened? It slowly came to me. While I was thinking that I may not get off this mountain, the Holy Spirit made his presence felt. God instantly brought to my mind that he was with me. Slowly, constantly the Holy Spirit made his

"Where are they now?"

presence known. That is the most important thing I could ever share with you. God, not I made my death peaceful. It was even enjoyable. As each moment progressed I thought more longingly about being with Christ. I experienced the filling of the Holy Spirit before I died, as I had many times during my previous 37 years. I was filled to overflow with God's spirit before I died. I remember looking at the beautiful view of Mount Rose. I remember looking at it and thinking Heaven must be even much more beautiful than even this. As I looked at my earthly surroundings I began to notice a couple of angels were with me. This did not startle me, I could feel God and Heaven wrapping around me. I felt more intensely the Holy Spirit of God. I was still seeing my earthly view of the mountain side, yet my sight was now seeing the angels and feeling the Holy Spirit. I then had this feeling of slipping out of my body. I noticed I could no longer move my arms or legs. It felt like how you feel if you ever ran out of gas. The whole car is unresponsive. With a car, you can't steer it or brake or use the radio or ac. You can't operate it. I had operated my body for 57 years, yet at this point I the operator, was separate from my body. I was also in the same dimension as I was in. I was still on the mountain but I looked forward and saw my body still strapped in to my seat belt. It did not bother me, my daughter's analogy of hearing "we are ghosts in a meat suit was perfect." My flesh was behind me; my body was not longer attached to me. This is also very important, I never felt dead and then alive. As my body was dying and then died, I never was unconscious. I was alive and then more alive. Now I was fully with the Holy Spirit. I felt so much love from him, towards myself. It was like being with someone you love but much more intense. I knew this fellowship with Christ was by far the best part of the afterlife. That is uninterrupted connection with the Lover of our soul. God is the top prize, the single by best part of being in Heaven.

We started walking on a new mountain. I did remember thinking "I feel so alive." I felt joy, excitement, extreme contentment.

Something else that comes to mind is I could tell that God really liked me. Did you know God really, sincerely likes us? I mean as friends. The bible says in John 15:15 Jesus is speaking "I no longer call you servants but friends…." Folks he has the feeling of friendship towards us. We also can be the friend of God. We have to stop from pushing God away and ask him for us personally to be born of the spirit. Did you know he deeply enjoys spending time with us?

Long before I died, I could feel how much God loved and liked me. I could feel that even more as God and I were walking through a new mountain meadow. In a short while I noticed people were coming up to us. It was my mom and dad. My grandmother and happily a nearly agnostic uncle as well came to greet me. They were all in their 70's and 80's when then died. Now they looked like they were in their 30's. My grandmother was born I think in 1903. When I died in 2023 she would be around 120 years old. Yet she looked like she was maybe 30.

They were all healthy looking and very friendly. They made me feel so welcome to be there. They all hugged me, now that was a feat in itself. We don't have flesh in Heaven, yet I could very much feel the hugs by my family. We just don't realize what capabilities we have with the spiritual body. I had more senses than I had here on earth. I had no

"Where are they now?"

sense that I was incomplete or just a ghost. I felt very much alive, and complete.

I did see something that also made me swell to bursting with joy. Now there were six of us walking. I noticed that the Holy Spirit had visibly left and now we were walking with Christ. As the Bible says no man can see him and live. Well I was dead now so I could see him. I could see his silhouette and he was very bright. Yet I could see him now as a man. He made me feel loved as we were walking. In a field I saw something else. As a lonely boy and as a grown man I had become very attached to my pets. During my life I had six cats and two dogs that I had felt close to. I had cried harder as a grown man when my two dogs died than when my parents had died. Just being lonely I had developed a closer relationship with them. My exact, specific pets that had died ran to meet me. That was more joy than I could even imagine.

I felt like my heart would burst just seeing and feeling my animals again. I guess it's a good thing I did not have a heart at the moment, it might have actually exploded. Another group of people came towards me. I had helped lead a few individuals to Christ. They and some of their friends and family were there as well to greet me. This was just the best time I had ever had in my life. Another surprise was a man came to greet me. I at once knew who this man was. Even though I had never met him, it was my son. He had been aborted nearly 40 years previously. I had not wanted to abort the baby but my girlfriend at the time said there was no other choice. It was fantastic to meet him. I thought I had been in Heaven for a long time. It seemed like days, even though there is no night or day there. After my son came to me shortly afterwards I felt pain for the first time and realized that was my body causing me pain. I really did not want to ever go back into my body. But I had no choice and off I went from Heaven and my loved ones back to a very cold, dark body storage cooler at Mount View Cemetery. That was a major disappointment.

Like many millions of people I had this NDE experience. At some point we come back. Many millions more die each year, and they do not come back.

All of us living and those who have died are born are placed on an invisible conveyor belt. We move though many similar and many different life experiences. We are all moving to the end of our own conveyor belt. Each human's life or conveyor belt is of a different length. Picture this, we are living and moving on the conveyor belt. The conveyor belt also has an invisible and very real exit on them.

Inside your body you are the operator. You are taking care of your body, or like many of us taking fair to poor care of it. You are making your body move. You articulate your body, like a puppet. You master or control your own body; you are the driver of your own vehicle. Since you were born, you are also using the computing power and knowledge in your brain. At human death, the operator exits their own body. Thousands and thousands of near NDE experiences, talk of immediately going downward through rock and dirt. The terror of being separated from your body and then being able to pass downward to the sides of the pit, that alone is overwhelming. The Bible describes Sheol or Hades as a pit. When Jack comes up to speak he will fill you in more on the pit.

"Where are they now?"

When I say Sheol is the absence of all good things let me add a little to that. Imagine a store that had everything. Like a Super Wal-Mart but more. Let's say it also had houses, cars, boats, and pets. It had a great jobs and spouses and friends in it. Let's say you over the course of your life, you purchased or acquired all the things and friends you want. Think of all the good memories you have had. The great views of nature you have seen. There are so many great things in life I can not name them all. Now imagine at death you lose them all. Plus you even lose control of your decision making. You go in to the Earth and have full knowledge of that is your new eternal home. As Jack will explain in a few moments how awful Hades is. Just add to that everything from your current life on earth is gone as well. The words devastating, heartbroken, despairing barely describe the sense of loss a person experiences that resides in Hades. That person got what they thought they wanted a life apart from the lover of their soul. Believe me that is the number one thing you WANT to have. You absolutely have to have Christ's acceptance and love. Some of the audience sat there looking a little deflated and somber. A Few said amen.

Okay I'll take a couple of questions. The pastor will give you a microphone. Frank pointed at a lady standing up, "Okay you ma'am, what is your question?" Why do some people who are not Christians see Heaven when they die? Frank replied, Okay you asked me the hardest question first. The Bible teaches the only way to get saved and be in Heaven is thru Christ. Of the millions, yes millions of NDE persons, they talk about seeing or feeling a barrier of which if they went over they could not have returned. A couple of different things are happening to non-believers as they have NDE. First they many times have the Hellish experience as it is commonly called. The other is God may be allowing them to see the Heavenly vision. It's an enticement to repent and be converted. God can take us from where we are to where he wants us to be spiritually. Giving a non-believer a positive Heavenly vision can lead a person to come to Christ.

Remember a near death experience is not death. I was clinically dead and still God brought me back.

The Bible says it's appointed for man to die once and then the judgment. A person could have multiple NDE. At some point they don't come back and they experience the afterlife completely. At that point there are only those who are saved by birth of the spirit as Jesus said be Born Again. The other group is those who leave everything good in this life at their death. Arriving and waiting in Hades until the Great White Throne Judgment. Scripture is clear Jesus said "if you deny me before others I will deny you before my father in Heaven." Many scriptures directly, specifically state as does this one Jesus say's "I am the way the life and the truth. No one comes to the father but through me." With that there was several Amen's and head nods. "Now I see many of you agreed with me. I also noticed some have blank expressions. If any of you want to be sure you're going to be with God and you're saved loved ones after you die, you can become sure now.

Before I pass the microphone to Jack I'm going to ask if any of you want the Holy Spirit to live with you so you can start that relationship now. So think about the question

"Where are they now?"

I'm going to ask you. You don't have to answer it out loud. Do you want to feel God is with you when you're all alone? This is important, a Christian feels and knows God is with them even when they are alone. Hay audience do you have that? If you don't have that connection to God you can get it. If your sins are not put under Christ's payment for your sins, then there is a separation between you and God. This separation is good to acknowledge. It's that main reason you fear death. Because God is telling you that he has a problem with you. He's letting you experience the unpleasant feeling you have of him being your Enemy. He wants to move us from the enemy group to the friendship group. In Colossians 1:21-23, God says "you who were once enemies he has now reconciled, now calling you friends. Each person wanting to go to Heaven has to accept God's conditions for that to happen. The Bible says if you believe in your heart and confess with your mouth that Jesus died for your sins and was resurrected that you will be saved from your sins. To believe that truth, God alone has to give you the faith to believe. When a non-believer dies they stop experiencing the many thousands of good things we are blessed with in this life. At death for an unsaved person they feel alone. Now that they are not in a body they go downward to a created place for the devil and his angels. That is the holding area of Hades. This all happens with full knowledge and comprehension of what is happening. The sense of terror and lose of control is unbearable.

Jack is going to come up here and talk about his NDE. Which as you may know was very different from mine. Good morning everyone. A couple of hands in the audience went up before Jack could continue,

CHAPTER 22

JACK'S SERMON

I will take some questions at the end of my testimony. This is my first time speaking to a large crowd so please be patient I was not born in a Christian home. Like some of you I grew up with two parents. Neither parent talked much about God. I went to a public school. Neither my parents nor teachers ever talked bad about God and the Bible. There was just no mention of either. In middle and high school I had girls flirt with me. Frank got his heart broke at 19. That was foreign to me I broke off things with girls if they got to clingy. Frank became a Christian at 20 because of that heart break. I was in maybe my 10th relationship by that age. All of which were fine. I just had the mindset if a relationship fell apart; there was another one available to me.

I finished high school and then attended college. I received a degree in marketing. I got a couple of jobs before I was realtor. When I became a realtor is seemed easy and I did well with it. I have been a realtor now for 20 years. I have made good money and life has been good. Looking back I also always had a fear of death. I did not know what

"Where are they now?"

to do about it. It started when I was maybe 12 years old and slowly grew bigger as I got in to my 20, 30's. At 40's it became bad. I had everything going for me so I kept shoving that fear feeling down in me. Every once in while I would hear a person talking about God or see some TV show about God. I really figured I did not need God. My parents and grandparents had done seemingly great and never mentioned God. When I was in my mid 40's one day I asked my 70 year old dad if he feared death. My dad said "son you just fear it because it's the end. You're afraid of the expected pain and the end of everything. You can't do anything about the fear of death. You just have to ignore it and enjoy your life. When you die everything stops and you feel and experience nothing." I left my dad that day feeling a little better. When I had that nagging fear of death I would just remember what my dad had said. When you die everything stops. Well, when I died on the hill after our van rolled. I learned what my dad thought and said about death was wrong. As I have now learned many thousands of people talk about their NDE. So far they all start the same. At death no matter how they die they are conscious. Even if a person is physically weak, their eyes may be closed they are aware of what is happening. I was very aware of what was happening even as I lay on the hill where I died. My eyes were closed and a very nice caring person named Alice was holding my hand. I could not respond to her but she was speaking to me. She had asked me moments before while my eyes were open if I "wanted to accept Christ." I whispered, "You know I don't believe in that and besides it's too late for that. I closed my eyes and expected to not experience anything. Here is where things got weird. Alice started saying Jack, Jack, Jack wake up. I heard an old man's voice near her saying "check his pulse." She now held my wrist. The old man held my other wrist. The old man let my hand go and said he's gone. Alice said yah I don't feel any pulse. What was weird at the time is, I heard them. There was never a time I felt nothing or my mind was blank. I expected to stop thinking, feeling etc. Instead I rose above my body and looked down. I was a couple of feet above Alice and the old man. There was even a long haired black cat with them. It had its paw on my foot. I could see my body there and I was no longer in it or connected to it. It was scary I could tell I was very much seeing and thinking about what was happening. I was very much now only the "me behind my eyes." It was just how Frank said death is like being in a car and running out of gas. You can still sit in a car when it stops but you no longer control it. When you die you cannot operate your body anymore but most importantly and GET this, you still exist. I began to go downward. I could not interact with Alice or the old man. The cat held eye contact and looked at me and watched me as I came from above them to ground level. Then I started descending into the ground and dirt itself. I moved effortlessly though dirt and rocks. It was scary and I could tell I had zero control. I kept trying to do something but there was nothing I could do. I knew I was not sleeping. This was not a dream. I was very aware that my body was dead. But, I the operator of the body was not dead. I was going downward, continuing towards somewhere. I had the thoughts I hope I'm not going to Hell. I had no thoughts of comfort. As I descended I only felt terror. I remember being filled with very, very large feelings of loss. I had paid off my house. I had a nice yard, three very nice paid for cars. I had

"Where are they now?"

enjoyed traveling and doing almost anything I wanted. I was reminded that I would never enjoy those good things again. I would never feel my dog lick my hand again. I would never feel a kiss from my wife again. I would never again have a hug or have my cat rub on my head while sitting on the couch. I would never see my dog wagging his tail at me. I would never see my dog happy to see me. I would never receive praises from any human again. I was aware that I was in a reality that had nothing good in it. I was aware that the Bible said God was the source of all good things. I had just thought that was a joke. That it was not possible. I now knew it was completely correct. I would never spend time with any of my friends or family again. Not only would I never eat food again, I would also never drink water or anything else again. I felt anger towards God, a huge overwhelming sense of lose. I also was feeling so much terror. That got worse as I continued going deeper into the earth. After a while I came through to a giant valley. It was as I now know called the pit. It was so huge, I was aware that no one on earth unless they had died knew this place existed. I hovered a few moments over this enormous cavern or pit. I looked down at the sides of this pit and it was rock. I realized the whole pit had many thousands or millions of what looked like odd sized openings or crude windows. I realized this rock pit was a building made of rock. After a few moments more I felt myself descending downward. I passed hundreds or thousands of floors downward of these cave windows. Sometimes I would see people or the souls of people looking out of the openings or windows. It instantly came to mind this was a huge prison or jail. I could see and hear people screaming. They screamed in terror and rage. They were scarred and very mad at God. I saw angels as well. They were more than twice as tall as a man. I'm guessing they were 12 to 15 feet tall. They stared me down as I entered into my own cell.

While I was there I was so miserable. I had no strength. Even though people in Sheol do not have bodies, the spirit body we have can move and has the same look as here on the surface. I'm 6ft 2 and I could not stand up in the cell without hitting my head. I'm guessing the cells were a little over 5 feet tall. In Sheol or Hades it is so hot. I asked one angel who was more reasonable how hot it was. The angel said "its way over 300 degrees up here. Several miles downward, towards the fire it's thousands of degrees." Then the angel gleefully volunteered "yah there are even more demons down there. The lower a prisoner is placed the smaller some of the cells are. Jack speaking to the audience said, so everybody I don't know if you want to hear more but there is more. So hold on. A couple of attendees got up. Jack continued. "Everyone is naked down there. There is nothing sexual about it. You just feel humiliated and possess nothing. No shoes, no underwear, not a pillow or blanket. You have no bed; there is no food or water. You don't need it. There are no cell phones, no TV's, no lights except from what I think is the lake of fire. But you very much want all those comfort things. But they are gone for all time. The sense of despair is overwhelming but there is nothing good coming, ever! Because God is the source of all good things and I had told him I didn't need him. Man was I wrong. Listen up every one, every human alive needs God and we knowingly or unknowingly receive every, I mean EVERY good thing from God that he allows us to steward during our lives.

"Where are they now?"

Every person down there is very alone. You don't talk to anyone, because everyone is separated. It's very noisy as well. All I heard was everyone crying and ragging. People went back and forth between sadness, loss and despair to ragging and screaming out of their cells or cursing at God. No one had lost their mind they were now in complete charge. All they shared was the worst that mankind has to offer hate, despair and loneliness.

I lay in my cell and had all those feelings as well. This is where God brought me encouragement. As I lay there, smelling the very real stench of sulfur I thought of mexican food. For the first time since my arrival in this Hell of Sheol I thought about God. I thought "thank you God for the good things I enjoyed while I was alive." Suddenly a demon "screamed what are you doing?" The demons instantly became enraged and started grasping at me and screaming no." The odd aspect of that was, I did not say the words yet somehow the demons knew what I had thought. With that I exited my cell and started going upwards. I began to feel encouraged for once. A few minutes later I woke up back in my body. I had never been so happy in my life to have left that place, and to be back on the surface of the Earth. Believe me there is a pit far, far below us. You never ever want to visit there. There are millions or perhaps billions of souls there at this very moment. Here is the best version up on the screen of what I see as being Sheol. As you can see from the overhead slide its enormously wide. It's even deeper than it is wide. It had consistent walls and shaping. Yet it also had many, many irregular caverns and turns. It was not shapped like a perfect circle but it was round. Like if you were to look down from a helicopter at a 100 mile long race track. It was irregular shaped but closer to a circle than any other shape.

I'll take a few questions now, if anyone has any from the audience. Frank was walking around the audience with a microphone. There were a few people with their hand up. Frank walked over to the first man with his hand up. Hello my name is Steve, my question is for Jack. What was the shape or height of his pit? Well that's a good question. How many of you know the distance from Reno to Carson City? Nearly every hand went up. How far is that? Shout out some answers. Everyone started shouting out 30 to 35 miles.

Jack replied, that's right, from downtown Reno to downtown Carson its 32 miles. When I arrived in Hades I came through the roof of it. I could see this massive valley. It was what I believe the Bible calls "the pit." When I first saw it I could tell a couple of things. One was it was a real place inside the Earth. I was never unconscious when I died. I had the very real validation that everything was real. This pit is down there at this very moment. The Bible is full of references to it being in the earth. When I hovered over this enormous pit, I was trying to process how large it was. It seemed about the size of the area between Reno and Carson. I had never seen a pit that size in my life. The next was the depth. It was deeper than it was wide. To us that is unheard of. But a massive cavern that size, miles and miles under ground is much less than half of one % of the Earth's mass. I'm guessing it was 40 miles deep. Again nothing like we have ever seen on the surface of the Earth. I say 40 miles because it was deeper than it was wide.

The audience just sat there stunned. Jack continued, "One math guy told me that's roughly the equivalent of a

"Where are they now?"

20,000 story building. I say levels or stories because it did have a rock opening seemingly for each jail cell. These windows went downward and horizontally. At some point I could not even see the windows because of the great distance. The same math guy said that if this jail was 100 miles in circumference (that's what a 30 mile wide circle valley would be) and if it were 40 miles deep at 20,000 levels it could hold many billions of people. I do remember an angel telling me with great glee that after the resurrection our spirit bodies will be reunited with our flesh bodies. Then the angel or demon said we will be down here in the pit with our resurrected bodies. That's very bad. It's so bad there and to add a supper 2.0 version of your body there makes it even worse.

You sir over there what is your question? The man replied, Thank you; "are you afraid of going back to Hell when you die?" Jack replied, "That became the most important question of my life after I came back. After I came back I was transported to one of our local hospitals. In the ambulance I had a nice lady beside me holding my hand. I said several times "please don't let me die, please don't let me die." I realize she could not stop me from dying if I was to go. But she said "We won't, we will have you to the emergency room in a few minutes. She told me my vitals were good. I fell asleep and woke up at the Hospital. I woke up and I was in my room. The first thing I thought of was "I need to get saved". I asked my nurse if she knew where the other passengers were. She said they had gone to all of the area's five major Hospitals. I asked who else was here at this hospital. She said she would find out. Well she did and said one of the people was Frank Locksley. I asked, "Can I could talk to him." In a matter of a couple of hours he and I were talking face to face there in the hospital. The moment I first saw him I blurted out "I need to get saved. I went to Hades and I don't want to ever go back there again. Frank said. Getting saved is not ONLY getting out of Hell. You have to believe in your heart that Jesus is God and that he was raised from the dead. You have to say that you accept him in front of other men. You can only do these things honestly if God gives you the faith to say them. Our faith is a gift of God. Unless he gives you faith you're not going to believe it or say it. Faith is not something you create; the word of God brings you faith. The word of God is actually alive. The word of God is living and stirs the reader's heart. Jesus said if you accept me then I will accept you. But if you deny me in front of others I will deny you in front of the Father. Faking it will not get you into a relationship with God." I interrupted Frank, Frank stop, I believe all that. Have you told or confessed that to other people? "No" I said sheepishly. Then do it right now. We sat there a couple of minutes then a cleaning person and a nurse walked in. I blurted out "Hay I believe Jesus died and that God the Father raised him from the dead. I believe what Jesus said and I want you both to know Jesus is God and Jesus has changed my life. The cleaning guy said that's great man. You will never regret it. There is nothing better than being right with God. The nurse said a little less enthusiastically that's great. Let me get your vitals. When I told these two people I felt freedom. I was not ashamed of Jesus; I wanted to tell others that Christ was my life now. I was not afraid to tell others about him. I felt his presence inside of me and I knew it was there. I had the arrival or the birth of the Holy Spirit in me or along side of me. It was and is very real.

"Where are they now?"

One little kid stood up and raised his hand. The pastor had a microphone and walked over to the boy. Pastor Tom asked him "What's your name and do you have a question for Frank or Jack? My name is Steve Lonovan. I'm 12 and wanted to ask Jack and Frank the same question, sure pastor Tom asked "what's your question?" Why do you think you and Frank came back? Pastor Tom asked which one of you wants to take that question. Jack answered, "hey Frank why don't you take this one." Okay sure replied Frank. I think God wanted us as he does all Christians to tell our testimony. If you have been born again believe me Christ wants you telling others about that experience. Jack and I are one of millions of people worldwide that have had NDE. Secular scientists call the term of what happened to us as being Auto resuscitation. This means we were clinically dead, and came back with no medical assistance. Also meaning there was no medical or scientific reason for our body to come back to life or we would not have been resuscitated. Speaking logically a dead body can do nothing to assist in coming back. The Bible says Christ holds all things and matter together. That includes our wonderful and frail bodies. If Christ had not done that then mine and Jack's bodies would be in graves and we would not be speaking to you. We were brought back to speak about Christ and also to love our family and friends. It's ironic that the souls in Hades would give anything to come back to their bodies. Conversely the souls in God's presence would not take anything to leave. Any of the people with a dead body on earth and their soul with Christ never wants to come back. Being with the lover of our soul IS Heaven. The high light of Heaven is God himself. Additionally, the place is beautiful and fantastic. God wants us to tell others that being in fellowship with the Holy Spirit is truly fullness of Joy. That full joy is available no were else. Just remember no one is going to Heaven unless it's thru Jesus. He is the great stumbling block. Those who push him away will stumble over him.

It's been said if Christians knew how fantastic being in Christ's full presence was, people would be walking in front of bus's everywhere. Folks please don't do that, but be encouraged when life is hard. Someday we will literally be in God's physical presence. Someday, we also will be in resurrected bodies that are like Jesus' body after his resurrection. Folks, I wanted to add to something Jack said. Jack was always aware. I was as well. In fact of the thousands of NDE reported worldwide there is a consistency. All the people that died and came back never felt dead and then alive. They felt their body dying and then felt much more alive. When NDE people leave their bodies they are aware of everything around them. They never turn off. Their bodies turn off but the soul or "meat suit operator" does not lose consciousness. Even many people who were "high" on a drug or very drunk on alcohol report instant sobriety at death.

Another person stood and wanted to ask a question. This time a deacon walked to this middle aged man. The deacon asked the man "what your name and what's your question?" My name is Glen, my question is for Jack. How many people do you think you saw or do you think were in Hell? With that Frank handed the microphone to Jack. Jack started. "Well that's an important question. I tried to figure that out. Two things came to mind, I had an angel or you could say demon answer that very question from me. "How many people are down here?" I asked. The demon actually responded. Many

"Where are they now?"

times the falling angels either scream at you or ignore you. Anyway the demon said "that is a question we like to answer. "We love discouraging humans. There are many, many of your family members down here. The best part, there are billions of humans down here. There is room for many more." With that the demon slammed his body into my cell window and then flew off. The cells were real rock I could not stand up in them. I'm guessing there was a complete cell every 10 ft. I had guessed the pit to be like 30 miles from one side to the other or 100 miles around and 40 miles high. If I was anywhere close to the mark there would be 528 cells per mile. That multiplied 100 miles in a circle would be 52,800 cells per level. Then with short cells going downward 40 miles would be 20,000 stories or levels. From my little view point it did look like the cells were roughly the same height and width as far as I could see. That's over 10 billion jail cells down there. So I would sadly say billions of people are down there.

During the last hour, there will be about 7,000 deaths worldwide. That's almost 2 per second worldwide. We all like to not think about that. But remember to the people who are dying they are very much thinking about it. Those same people are usually either terrified and then drugged. The Christian group are usually making sure they are truly connected to the Holy Spirit and then enjoying their connection with God. Another group is what I like to call the "worrying what's about to happen group" Thiers does not need much explaining. A preacher once said we should not think of those who are in Hades now without a tear coming to our eye. Folks we got to get serious about soul wining. Jesus said the way is narrow and few there are that find it. Jesus also said I am the way the truth and the life no man comes to the father except through me. We got to help folks focus and cling to Christ. He is the life jacket to make it off the sinking ship of life. He's the only way. Every other way leads to the Pit of Hades, literally.

Jack said thanks folks, the audience clapped. Okay folks I'm going to hand the microphone back over to Frank and he has a couple of more things to say. Then we will wrap up this service. Thanks to all of you for coming. We will hang around after services let out and we will be able to talk to you all out in the court yard. Jack got many more claps and amen's from the audience. Frank started again. I'm not going to talk a lot now. I know that may be hard to believe. I was just going to piggyback on some of what Jack so honestly said.

I and Jack had a NDE. The letter N stands for the word near. We both did not cross over the barrier of which there is no coming back. Unfortunately close to 7,000 people per hour die every hour on this planet of 8,100,000,000. That's very close to 2 human deaths a second. Watch this 20 second video. The brief video played. Okay now in that video you just saw one person pass in twenty seconds. Again in real life 40 people just died in the last 20 seconds.

Once again here is my conveyor belt video. 2 humans a second are coming off the belt and going into the afterlife. Jesus said most people are not going to Heaven. Most are going to Sheol and eventually Hell afterward. In Heaven we will be with our creator and any feeling of inferiority will instantly disappear. We will never feel those negative feelings again. Lastly I like to add an analogy I heard from my daughter. She asked me years ago. "Daddy are we ghosts living in a meat suit". I thought about it and said we are. The

Jews taught our body is the interface with the decision making soul of a person. At death the soul or operator slips out of the "meat suit" and begins the afterlife as Jack's death was or as mine was. If anyone out there does not have assurance that when you die you will be in Heaven, now is the time to act. The Bible says in 2nd Corinthians 6:2 "That NOW! Is the acceptable time to be saved. Don't wait to be saved. As the saying goes you may think "I'll wait until 11:59 pm to be saved," only then to die at 10:30 pm. If the Holy Spirit is pulling on your heart, don't ignore it. Or that is better said ignore the Holy Spirit. God's pulling on your heart is not something you may always feel. The more you ignore his calling the less you will notice it. If you continue to ignore it, at some point you may not feel his call anymore. Then you may not be able or interested in responding to Christ. Do you have the Holy Spirit living in you? Can you feel the Holy Spirit in you, and surrounding you now? If not, you can change that. Just as Jack believed and told others you must believe in your heart and confess with your mouth that Jesus is Lord and that he died and was raised from the dead.

The pastor is going to come up here and if any you want to move from being an enemy of God to his loved one and a friend then come up here right now. The pastor will lead you in a prayer. Five people came up and stood there. It was fantastic to see these five souls accepting and believing on Christ for Salvation.

Frank interjected "Those of you that have done this today, God Bless you! You can rejoice that your name is now written in the Lamb's Book of Life. Go talk to the pastors, telling them of your new conversion. They can give you resources to help you start your new life in Christ. If any of you want to talk with Jack or me afterwards, we will be out in the court yard after this service. Thank you. The pastor came up and said a prayer of blessing over the congregation and then the worship music started and everyone was dismissed and started getting up to leave the sanctuary.

Frank and Jack stood outside. Frank told Jack "I think that went well." Before long there were about 200 people surrounding them both. It was flattering and intimidating. A reporter from a Christian TV network came through the crowd and yelled out a question. "Mr. Locksley is it hard to be back here in the land of living when you were in the presence of Christ. How do you handle not seeing those loved ones who greeted you in Heaven? Frank started," I admit it was very much a letdown to come back among the dying. I call Heaven the land the land of the living. I'm very happy to see my wife and daughters again. The rest of everything is always better in Christ's presence. Something we think of us is we are here and God's somewhere else. God the Father, Son and Holy Spirit exist in both realms. We exist here now in the eternal, spirit realm. We just don't see it. All I have to do is as my son in Heaven told me is look at Jesus. Jesus currently is watching us. I also think of the love he had for everyone including me back at the crucifixion. I can see him looking at me with the eyes of love. Even while he was on the cross, his love for me and everyone is constant. We are never out of his loving gaze. At this very moment he is thinking of us all. He constantly reminds me that I am in his presence. If I sin and he is grieved he has told us how to restore the intimacy. Intimacy with the Holy Spirit makes every challenge of this Earth much easier to look

"Where are they now?"

past. The main prize of Heaven is closeness and fellowship with Christ. Thanks everyone have a blessed day."
 Jack cheekily said folks get ready for Jesus. He's coming back. Ask yourself are you excited? Or are you scared. Your feelings can tell you a lot. You can measure how aware you are spiritually and what you may have to change. Jack then waved and walked out of the court yard.

CHAPTER 23

"CONSTRUCTION CHAOS"

Frank and Jack were both enjoying a leisurely day off. Frank and his wife were fixing some lunch for their family. Frank is dragging a hose around to water his grass. They had lived in their home for 30 years. During that time Frank had thought they needed a sprinkler system many times. Yet he had never installed one. He also had never had someone else install a sprinkler system.

Jack at Franks suggestion was watching "Somewhere in Time" with his wife. He was enjoying some of the movie. Jack had been falling asleep during the movie as well.

Frank and his wife put in a family movie and began watching. Back at Jack's house he and his wife had dozed off.

Jack is startled by a phone call from the lead Chaplin. Jack and Frank had volunteered to help spiritually with those who may be in life threatening circumstances. The chaplain tells Jack there has been a construction collapse accident. There are dozens of wooden five story apartments under construction around the city. That was the local legal

"*Where are they now?*"

limit to how tall building contractors could build a building without having to use steel or concrete. Anything with more floors had to have steel or steel and concrete in the support columns under the wood stories. John the lead chaplain tells Jack. "Hay I'm on my way to the construction accident site. The local police called me and said there are some trapped men. Some of them are asking for prayer. Can you meet me there and help out for a few minutes." Jack replied "I can be there in about 10 minutes." Jack whispered to his listening wife "It will take more than a few minutes" "Yah" laughed his wife, "try hours." Go ahead I got my class calendar and student art to plan." Jack went and grabbed his Bible and some comfort tracks and a few gospel tracts. He climbed into his truck and drove off. On his way he called Frank. Frank answered "hay man, what's up" "John called and said he wanted some help at a construction accident," replied Jack. Frank said "Yah, I just got a text from him. I'm driving there now. Oh and I threw an extra pair of steel toed boots in my van, just in case you needed them." Thanks I'll see you at the site, replied Jack. While Frank was driving he got a call from Alice. Frank asked, "Alice, how are you? "I'm good and a little confused replied Alice. We'll I can't talk much now Jack and I are going to a construction site collapse. Can we talk later asked Frank? Sure, where is the collapse at? "The collapse is in the North Valley, across the street from the Wal-Mart Supercenter." I just drove past that, can I turn back and help out, asked Alice. Sure, just don't tell John I asked you to help, replied Frank. "Who is John", asked Alice. He is the lead chaplain; he's our chaplain volunteer boss. "Okay, how can I help, what do I do," asked Alice.

"Just look for Jack and me. We are both wearing bright yellow volunteer vests.

It was a large 300 unit 10 acre construction site. The building was framed and now they had been adding the roof. The interior electrical and plumbing was being installed. There was very little dry wall or siding installed. This building was seven stories, retail space and parking was on the bottom and then all parking on the second floor. The top five stories were wood. When Alice got to the construction site it was chaotic to say the least. There was one REMSA vehicle and one police car on site. She could hear more of both on their way. She quickly started looking for Jack and Frank. After walking around the site she looked to where there was a group of construction workers huddled. It was at the entrance to one of the buildings. She walked toward the group and then saw Frank and Jack. Jack saw her and ran over to meet her. Jack had been very grateful to Alice since after the van rollover accident. She had been instrumental in Jack coming to Christ. Jack said "hay you might have to help some of these construction workers cross over." Raising her eyebrows, "That's not funny or good. Is it that bad here, asked Alice. In unison, Yah it is replied Frank and Jack. Frank had just walked by Jack on his way to Alice. "Alice you can help, but keep it kind of low key. We can comfort people and converse about God. But they want us to be kind about it." "I will be respectful and kind, replied Alice. I know you will that's why I said you could help". Jack said let's say a quick prayer, Alice and Frank leaned in. "Lord let us help these people and give us wisdom to say the right words. In Jesus name, then they all three said Amen at the same time.

"Where are they now?"

John the lead chaplain pulled up and Jack and Frank walked up to meet him. Frank asked John "where do you want us." Let me ask the construction foreman, I'll also check in with the police captain, replied John. After a quick check with both the construction foreman and captain, telling him the following "15 men have been injured. 6 of which had been pinned under debris. Two of those had been pulled free. John went over to Frank, Jack and Alice. He recapped to them about the injuries. "So we got 4 workers still pinned. Let's get to them, assess their physical and mental state. Then we can see how we can help." The group of chaplain volunteers could now see several little groups of construction workers grouped together. The construction workers were franticly moving around and yelling. The whole scene started to remind me of the 90's TV show called ER. The TV show was chaotic with nurses and doctors running from one patient to the next. On the show they were saving lives and losing others.

Not knowing what to do first, the group of us volunteer chaplains looked around. The three of us moved over to a group of construction workers huddled. We assumed that must be where a trapped construction worker was.

CHAPTER 24

TEETER TOTTERING; BETWEEN ETERNAL LIFE AND ETERNAL DEATH.

It would not take long before the three volunteers where busy, very busy. As they walked toward one group of huddled construction workers John handed Frank, Jack and Alice each a two way radio. They turned them on and there was a lot of chatter on them. They started walking quickly to the first group. It took a little work to get to the trapped first guy. "Hay move guys these chaplains have to get to Lamar. Lamar was a big muscular guy. He was pinned so deeply in the rubble that only his voice could be heard. No one could see him. While he was trying to be found, workers were trying to remove debris away from a giant pile of collapsed mangled wood. The pile on him also had mangled water and sewer lines. "I got his foot, Hay Lamar can you move you right foot asked Jack. "Yah man I can move it. Are you getting me out of here?" No man there are some search and rescue guys working on that right now. I'm just a weenie chaplain, replied Jack. Lamar asked, so are you here because I'm going to die? Do you think I'm going to

"Where are they now?"

die? Well I don't think you are going to die. You are going to die. Hopefully it's just not today, said Jack. You're not very good at comforting people are you, asked Lamar. Well that depends on a person's view point. Are you ready for what actually happens when you leave your body? Most people are not. I died myself and was dead for several hours. I had no relationship with Christ at the time. I spent the worst time of my life in a place many call Hell. It was actually Hades a torturous prison for all those waiting to go into the Lake of Fire of Hell. I can tell you Lamar if you're not forgiven by the King of kings, dying today will be the least of your worries. Your and my life is a waste if we let ourselves go to Hell. Lamar was quiet, Jack asked, how about if we get you right with the Lord. These men out here are working to save your body.

Suddenly Alice and Frank started calling for Jack. Lamar asked "hey man where are you going?" Jack replied I'll be right back, another chaplain named Alice is going to sit with you. She's just grabbed on to your hand now. She's great and a little nicer than I am. "Hey Lamar, how are you doing? Tell me a little about you," asked Alice. "I'm Okay. Jack was just giving me the get right with God speech. I did not have a chance to tell him I accepted Christ when I was 8 years old. But I do appreciate Jacks enthusiasm." "Jack can be a little direct. He died almost about a year ago. He came back and feels very compelled to tell people about getting saved. Is there anything I can do while the search and rescue remove this ruble? Yah can you call my wife and tell her I am okay. I can't reach my cell phone to call her. I would be happy to replied Alice. What's your wife's name? Kali, she's been calling me the last hour and half. Yah just tell her

I'm okay. I will, I'm calling her now. Kali his wife answered, "Hello Kali, my name is Alice, and I'm volunteer chaplain. I'm with your husband Lamar now. He wanted me to tell you he is okay. He can't reach his phone, but he wanted me to call you. He is currently pinned at the construction site." "Yah I know, I'm at the front gate now. They won't let me in," replied Kali. Go to the orange back gate and you can walk through there. Be careful walking, Alice can get you from there over to me, chimed in Lamar. Okay I'm walking over to that back gate now. It will take a minute. I'll go meet her at that gate and bring her back over here, added Alice. Thank you I'll be okay replied Lamar.

Alice headed over to what she thought was the area of the back gate. This construction site is bigger than I thought it was she mumbled to herself. A familiar voice replied "it is a big place you want to take the first right at the tractor up there and then left at the water tank and then you will be at the gate. Alice turned to see the same old man who had helped her nearly a year ago at the van roll over site. It's nice to see you. Why are you here? She asked. I help out with stuff like this. Wow! I was just thinking about you this morning, thank you so much for all the help you gave back at the rollover accident. I could not have made it without you and your cats help. Thank you replied the old man. I'll talk to you later said Alice. She quickly followed the old man's instruction and made it to the back gate. Kali was there waiting for her. The two walked quickly, carefully back over to Lamar. Okay Lamar I found your wife. I'll leave you two here. These search and rescue people are working hard to get you out of here. You are going to be okay Lamar. I will be back shortly. We have three other trapped workers here as

"*Where are they now?*"

you may know. Who is it, asked Lamar. Frank's voice crackled over the radio. Its three guys named Ren, Raj and Juan. Lamar shouted out, "Oh man you got to help those guys. I think they are all agnostics. Don't let them die man. Jack said we will do our best but we are not doctors, we are realtors. We are volunteer chaplains. Everyone chuckled. Don't make me laugh it's too painful while I'm pinned under this wood, chuckled Lamar.

Alice quickly ran to over Juan. Frank was there. Where is Jack, Alice asked. He's with a guy named guy named Juan replied Frank. How can I help, asked Alice. Frank replied "Why don't you go visit Raj. He's next to a tipped over cement truck." "Okay I saw that earlier. I'll go there now." Alice ran carefully though the messy site. On her way she saw the old man again from last year's van rollover. She waved at him and he waved back. The old man was seemingly heading to where Frank and Juan were.

Alice felt her now "clicky" hip acting up. Now sometimes when she walked her hip clicked. It even bound or would not swing a full walking stride. "I hate when my hip does this" she would say. Since the van roll over her hip hurt more often than not.

Alice got over to Raj. She started a conversation with him. "Raj can you hear me?" Yes, who are you?" I'm Alice a volunteer chaplain helping out today. Tell me about yourself Raj." "I will not talk to a woman. Get me a man to talk to." "I'll see what I can do", replied an irritated Alice. She stepped back and called Jack on the radio. "Yah Raj, will not talk to a woman. So can you come and talk with him?" "Okay it will be a couple of minutes. They just got a guy named Ren free. They are going to take him to the hospital.

They said he is in critical condition. He was talking a lot about Budda. As soon as he loaded up, I'll come over to where you are", replied Jack. Alice asked so does critical meaning he is dying? Not necessarily answered Jack. He just has not stabilized, the medic told me, so they call his status critical. Okay help me when you can. I'll sit with Raj until you get here.

Frank was with a guy named Juan. Juan can you speak English? Juan said yeah probably better than you do. English is my first language. Spanish is next. Sorry, I just don't know much Spanish, replied Frank. "It's no problem gringo. What do you want? Well I want you to tell me about you self, asked Frank. While I'm here, your co-workers and the hasty team are working to get you free of this collapse building." You are not here to help gringo? Well I'm here for you to talk to or if you need me to contact any friends or family members." Are you a priest or something, asked Juan? No I'm a volunteer chaplain, answered Frank. Why are you a volunteer you must not be serious about helping sick people, asked Juan? "Well that's a good question. About a year ago I died. I was dead for several hours. I saw Jesus immediately. Before my death, I could truly, heavily feel and then see the Holy Spirit. During that time I saw both my earthly surroundings and parts of Heaven. There were beautiful flowers, fields and mountains in this part of Heaven. After a while I was only seeing Christ and many dead saved family members. Juan, I very much love my family here on earth. Still I did not want to come back. I want all people to be okay when they die. It's very personal to me and to God that people be right with him at and even more importantly before they die." Juan just sat there with a blank half smile on his face.

"Where are they now?"

Frank impatiently now asked "is a relationship with God something you have or are interested in?" "Why do you ask that? I have gone to church since I was a little boy", replied Juan. That's good is God the most important person in your life. Do you cling to him for dear life? Is God the center of your universe? Is he the only way to get to Heaven? Is Christ more important to you than Heaven itself? Do you know the word of God? Most importantly do you know the God of the Word? Is Christ, the Father and the Holy Spirit everything to you? Is that God head even more important than your family, job or life? Do you know our own daily sin brings grief and separation between us and God? Do you wrestle with any of these issues? Or, does everyday life crowd out all of this from your thoughts?" Frank liked to overwhelm people with questions.

Why do you ask such questions? These questions do not bring me comfort, snapped Juan. Frank spoke softly; sorry since I died and came back my perspective has changed. If a person is getting close to dying, I as a chaplain or minister need to do more than help move the deck chairs on the sinking Titanic. If people are going to die they need more than hearing "everything is going to be okay". As my friend Jack will tell you, who just showed up. More times than not at a person's death, something very awful happens.

Okay, okay you are right! Jack jumped in, "hay bro are you a religious weenie? I say weenie because you're a Christian fraud. Hay man you got to be talking to the God who made you. If you're too cool or proud to be with God, Jesus will not acknowledge you in front of his Father.

You better get right and get God's spirit in you, now. Because if you die without him, you Juan, will go into a godless existence when you die. I know that because I did, and there are thousands of others who have died and come back and talked about the same awful truth. Juan looked a little nervous, Frank added "Or you can experience something like I experienced. I met Christ and many of my saved family and friends. I feel pressured, I don't like that, Juan blurted. Frank said "yah it's better to deal with the pressure now than to have unending regret after you die. About then the hasty team got the last of the debris off of Juan. Okay guys let us get him on a gurney. Frank and Jack stepped away from the team and let them load up Juan. While they were pushing Juan to an ambulance Juan yelled out thanks guys to Jack and Frank. "You're welcome, we will see you later," they both yelled back.

CHAPTER 25

THE REST OF THE STORY.

Juan, was getting loaded into a bus. Ren was also getting loaded up in to a bus. Lastly Raj had been recovered and had already been loaded up into a third ambulance. He was almost to the hospital. The lead chaplain radioed; Jack, Frank and Alice. "Hey you guys did a good job. Ren, Raj and Juan are all free of the collapse and going to area hospitals. I'm thinking you should go see them later today. They all are in critical condition. They are not stable but the medics believe they will advance to stable. I want you three to go visit them." We will leave now, which hospital are they going to, asked Jack. Two are going to Renown and one to St. Mary's. I would wait maybe an hour. So, they can get to the hospital, get any more treatment and into their rooms, replied the lead chaplain.

Let's go check on Lamar before we go, Alice said. Walking and weaving through the complex took a couple of minutes. "It's so quiet committed" Frank. 'Lamar is just around the next building there" blurted out Jack. Around the next corner was a group of small group of Hasty team members also known as SAR (Search and Rescue) there were also maybe a dozen construction co-workers. "Why are some of them they just standing there," asked Alice. Frank, Jack and Alice picked up the pace and walked the rest of the way to where Lamar was. It was still kind of quiet. "Why is Lemar still here," Frank asked a Hasty worker. Even though Lemar is mostly free, He's pinned from the waist down. The construction debris shifted and pinned him more and it started a lot of bleeding. His femoral artery seems to be damaged. As you can see we are working carefully to stabilize the collapse, replied the SAR captain.

I see you Lord; the Holy Spirit is here I can see him. I see angels. God loves us all so much. Lamar whispered. This is wonderful.

"Dude are you alright? Why are you talking crazy," one of his concerned buddies asked him. "Your mind is going south." It's beautiful here, God's is surrounding me. He loves us so much. Lamar answered. "Hey Lamar prove to me you're not crazy. What is calculus?" "Lamar said; it's the study of how much a function's slope changes at a single point, or its instantaneous rate of change. I'm more focused on the beauty of my new surroundings. The Holy Spirit and Jesus are here right now. I'm seeing here and there, it's so beautiful, Christ's love is wonderful." His friend asked "what do you mean here and there." Jack and Frank knew what Lamar meant. Frank said "Lamar is feeling and seeing the Lord's presence and glimpse of Christ's glory. He is also seeing and aware of his surroundings here at this construction site. He's in the doorway of death. For the Christian this is glorious and wonderful." Lamar whispered he's right. Lamar now was just smiling. The medic checked he

"Where are they now?"

no longer had any pulse. Lamar's wife was crying, holding Lamar's hand and partially smiling.

Whew! Jack said as they started to walk away. "Let's go see the other three" "Alright" Frank said. No I'm going to stay with the wife Alice replied. Alice walked a couple of feet and stood beside Lamar's wife. She reached over and held her hand. They both half smiled at each to other. They both started tearing up as well.

Frank and Jack got into Jack's truck and sped off towards the hospital. Mercy me's song "Cannot Say Enough" was playing on the stereo. They hit repeat on the hallelujah chorus a couple of times. Lamar is feeling this song now said Frank.

CHAPTER 26

ALICE RETURNS

A couple of days after the construction collapse, Alice felt restless. It had been nearly a year since the van roll over. It had changed many people's lives. It had a strengthening effect on Alice. She had gained some clarity. Her mind was more focused on telling others of her experience. Alice had told more of her friends and family members about the rollover accident experiences. Some people were interested and others seemed like she was annoying or scaring them. Even at other times her listeners showed some interest and annoyance simultaneously. It seemed important to her to tell others of death and what is happening on the other side.

To help encourage herself she thought she would take a drive to see the nice old man and cat who had helped her. She had just seen the old man a few days earlier at the construction site collapse. She decided to drive the nearly 20 miles from her home to the old man's home. The drive was all paved except for the last two miles being a dirt road. She knew exactly where his home was. She could feel herself

"Where are they now?"

being filled with excitement as she drove the last part on the dirt road. She drove to the little creek. She also remembered the house was next to two giant rocks and three giant trees. She had remembered it being called the 1, 2, 3 house. In front of the drive way to the house, was the one creek, two huge rocks and lastly three very tall trees.

When she got there it was all the same. The creek, two rocks and the three tall trees were there. Yet, there was no driveway, no barn and no house. She looked around and was confused. She did see the old man's International truck. It had the same license plates on it. She walked up and looked at the truck. It had a rotted out interior. The truck was missing the hood. There were large sapling trees coming up though the open hood. The saplings were large at least several years old. There was also no motor where the motor should be. She had remembered the shinny old man's engine in under the hood last year when she was there.

"How can this be?" she whispered to herself. She looked all around thinking maybe she must have missed seeing the house and barn. She walked slowly about a football field length towards a nearby house. Alice saw an old couple outside working on their garden. "Excuse me" both the old man and the women turned to look at Alice. "Hi my name is Alice; I was here about a year ago. I was part of the van rollover accident. I was one of the passengers in the van." The old couple looked at her and said "we do remember that terrible accident." "Alice continued, I walked from the rolled over van over to a house nearby. Then a nice old man and a cat met me. The old man was very kind and drove me back to the crash site. He grabbed nice couch cushions off his couch. We used the couch pillows at the crash site to make comfortable some of the passengers. I wanted to say hello and thank you to the man. He also had a sweet cat. Can you tell me where he is, or where he has gone?"

The old couple looked at her oddly; "well we have lived here over 30 years. There has not been a house near us for all those years." Alice now looked at them oddly. The old women continued, we do remember the accident, we both even remember seeing a women walking around over near that old creek. I think it must have been you. Alice said, "It probably was me;" Alice took out her cell phone and showed a picture of the outfit she was wearing that day. The old couple agreed and said "yes that is what she was wearing. Alice knew they were right because that was the last time she had worn that outfit. Alice could even now remember a old man and a women looking at her when she was there during the van rollover accident day.

The three of them felt uncomfortable, Alice said "well I'm going to go back over to the crash site and check it out. Thank you for your time." She got back in her car and drove the nearly 2 miles over to the crash site. The last few hundred yards she walked. It was too rough to get her car all the way there. As she drove and walked she had glimpses or flashbacks of the accident day. She remembered the game, the nice lunch, the time souvenir shopping up at Virginia City. She also thought of the mine tour and cemetery visit. It had been a nice day up until the accident. Then she remembered the emotional pain she felt from the crash. She remembered seeing her friends unconscious, she remembered going for help and the old man who helped her. "Everything was real but the old man, his cat and the

"Where are they now?"

house I imagined. That can't be." She walked around where the large van had come to a stop. She saw a square dark shape; she walked over closer to it. It was one of the pillows that the old man had brought with him. For the next few minutes she looked around and managed to see and gather 5 pillows that the old man had taken to the crash site the day of the crash. "I didn't lose my mind. The old man had brought the pillows from his living room couch." She had ridden with the old man, in his truck hauling those very same pillows. "I held these same pillows on my lap in his truck." This was all too real for her. Being a Christian she came to the conclusion the old man must have been an angel. No other explanation worked. Alice walked around the crash site for maybe an hour. She looked for other items of her co-workers and friends. She found a couple of their hats. There was the winning softball from the game they had played the day of the accident. It had all the signatures from her teammates on it. She looked at the signatures of those who were now dead. She shed some tears, she continued looking and remembering her friends. She even found the intact cell phone of her friend Sophie. That brought on more tears. She thought for a moment what splendid experience Sophie must be having at this very moment. Alice felt peaceful and content as she thought of Sophie visiting with Christ. She could think Sophie was visiting with friends and family she loved. She could only imagine how beautiful the scenery was. Alice remembered the time a man said his pets came up to greet him during his NDE. She envisioned Sophie seeing her pets surrounding her in a field of flowers. She knew now that it is all real. She smiled as she continued to think of Sophie's current activities.

With a satisfied look Alice slipped Sophie's phone into her pocket. Alice then thought of all the handholding and kind, encouraging words she had offered there that day. She had seen so many people's lives change that day. She was there as Sophie took her last breath. Alice had heard Sophie say Au revoir. She looked very much forward to seeing her good friend again in the future. She was there as Jack died. Alice had discovered Frank dead body. The shock of seeing many of your friends and co-workers bloody and unconscious was powerful. Alice was a Christian herself. She knew her co-workers and she knew some that died were in Heaven with loved ones and others were not. Both the believer and the unbeliever got what they thought they thought they wanted in the afterlife.

CHAPTER 27

WRAPPING IT UP, OR NOT.

Alice slowly walked back to her car. She was puzzled as to what the meaning of the old man not being there was. The fact that there was no sign he was ever there was a mind blowing concept. She also thought about the several events that had happened since the roll over happened.

Alice was also glad Jack and Frank had come back from the dead. Since the accident Jack and Frank had both stopped practicing real estate full time. They had shared the construction collapse challenge. Jack and Frank still held their real estate licenses. They sold houses every now and then. They both were working on writing a book. Frank was doing a little public speaking about his going to Heaven experience. He was even working on his getting his previous book "Titanic Fact and Faith" book converted into a short bible study training movie.

While Jack was working on his very own NDE experience book, he would sometimes speak at a same event as Frank. Alice thought It would be nice to go visit them and catch-up. Alice had thrown herself into her sales position and had sold more homes during the last year than in her previous years. She found herself talking about the accident even with potential home sellers and buyers. It was kind of therapeutic and it formed a quick connection to her new clients. They would list or buy homes with her because she had a depth to her. Alice sat in her car in the cool of the shade. It was pleasant out and she saw a cute bunch of baby bunnies going in and out of a rabbit hole. She fell asleep thinking I feel just like Alice in "Alice in Wonderland" She thought to herself, I wonder what will with the rest of my life. She was reassured as she fell asleep that the Holy Spirit was there with her. She woke up 45 minutes later; it's time to go home she said to herself. She primped herself in the rear view mirror. Starting the car she kept the radio off for a change. She got back on the dirt road and headed back to the main road. She turned left to go back down the hill towards Reno. Several miles down the road she saw a car that had rolled. It had just rolled over may be once. There were already a couple of sheriffs' vehicles on site. She slowed down and asked if they needed any help. No mam a deputy replied. We have several people helping. She once again saw the old man in his fancy old international. She wanted to get out and talk with him. She wanted to get to the bottom of why his home was not back where it was a year ago. She tried parking along the narrow road and several deputies told her "sorry ma'am you can't park here. Alice said "okay then please let me give you my phone number and give it to that old man helping. They said sure we will give him your number. You can't stay here sorry, replied the deputy. Alice mumbled to herself, "This is crazy what in the blazes is going on with that old man. Alice drove on down

"Where are they now?"

to RC Wiley's. She thought I'm going to check out their TV sale. My TV at home is so old and they have good prices here. While Alice was looking at several different TV's a news alert came on, "breaking news, six car pileup north of Las Vegas. A reporter came on live from the site. Hi this is Samantha Jones, I'm at the site of the six car pileup. Local law enforcement is on the scene. I have an eyewitness here who assisted accident victims before the police arrived. Sir, please tell me what you saw. Well, I was actually sitting in my old truck at the rest stop across the street when I saw the accident happen. Alice looked up at the wall of TV's; she looked to hear an old man's voice that sounded familiar. No it can't be her eyes locked on the TV. That's not possible I just saw and talked to the old man. He was here in Reno at the single car roll over. That was maybe 30 minutes ago. She glanced at her cell phone; It's has been 25 minutes since she saw the same old man in person. He and the cat were now in Las Vegas. That is 450 miles away. Alice stood there staring at the old man. The old man's cat jumped into his arms. The cat even reached out for the TV camera almost taunting Alice. Shaking her head Alice said 'it can't be, it can't be, no man can move that fast.

Here are a couple of my evangelism stories. Losing a friend, helping a few turn to Christ.

In the main story I talk about meeting a friend of the family named John in Heaven. Here is a brief part of his conversion story. I helped to be a part of that conversion. I have a few other quick stories unrelated to the main story. But they are a testimony of some conversions I was a part of. Something that I experience as do many believers is losing some of my friends. I became a Christian at the age of 20. I talked to my small sphere of influence. I began talking about Christ and that he was the God who had saved me. Most people gave me the deer in the headlight look or outright shake their heads at me. I had a couple of friends who were interested. One friend who I talked to several times converted. I was a zealot but ignorant on how to help bring people to Christ. I did not know how to speak the truth in love. That is probably the biggest reason I did not lead more people to Christ as a young Christian.

One friend after we had talked for a couple of hours, we decided to go each back to our own homes. We had been talking about what it means to be saved. This friend, was interested. When we were saying our goodbyes, I said think about this. When you are home go in to your bedroom and ask God to come into your life. I then said "If you believe in your heart and confess that Jesus Christ is Lord and that God raised him from the grave you will be saved." A few days later I saw that friend, and he said he had prayed to God privately in his bedroom and he believed and confessed that same truth. For the last 38 years that person has been walking with Christ.

"Where are they now?"

He told me a few times in the last nearly 40 years that was when he became a Christian. Being kind, respectful and patient when sharing your faith will get you much closer to bringing a person to the Lord. Don't damage the person or your relationship with them. As farmers will say it's important to not bruise the fruit when trying to pick it. Don't bruise a non-Christian while trying to lead them to the Lord. Speak the truth in love. And I have learned you should and need to tell people hard things. Jesus said you must be born again to enter the Kingdom of God. An unloving Christian may say turn or burn" That really helps very little and sounds like hate speech to a non-born again, unbeliever. The theology is correct but that wording and approach will turn most any un-believer away from drawing near the Lord. You want people to be drawn to God, not run the other way. I like what Pastor Greg Laurie says. "To win some you have to be winsome." Be attractive with the Gospel and things of God and people will become attracted to the things of God.

I would try for years working on other friends and family members to lead them to Christ. They would listen at first and then usually recoil like I was feeding them poison. I did get better at my approach. I really had to have love and respect for the person I was talking to. When I respected them as a person, even if I disagreed with them, the conversations were more productive. I did have a good friend in High school.

After High school, when I was 20, I became born again. As some call it a "born Againer" many just call that a Christian. Sadly many people who call themselves

Christians have not had the Holy Spirit born in them. So they are Christians in name only. God does not have fellowship with them. You cannot make yourself a Christian. God himself has to place his Holy Spirit upon you or along side of you. You can ONLY get that to happen when God gives you the faith to believe that Jesus is God and that the Father raised him from the dead. Until Christ does that work you are not a Christian and you are not saved from separation from God. Literally you are God's enemy until you are saved. My good High school friend called me when he was drunk. I was 24 at that time. I was thrilled that he had called me. It was some work for him to find my phone number. In 1991 he drove to my parents' house visited with them. Then he got my home phone number and gave me a call. I was excited because we were good friends in high school. He had a growing life and I had wife and a daughter. I figured we would pick up where we left off. Over the phone he told me about what he was doing with his life. I was listening and encouraging to his plans. I told him about my wife and daughter. We had just purchased my grandmother's house. He was supportive as well. I then told him about me becoming a Christian. He was now overly quite. I told him how wonderful it was for me. I never pushed Christ on him. I knew firsthand how people get nervous about the name above all names. Even just his name causes Joy and fear in the hearing. Well the conversation became uncomfortable. I even quickly stopped talking about Christianity. I switched back to his interests. He quickly wrapped up the call and now for 33 years he has never called me again. I have other friends from the past that never want to talk about Christianity or death. You can talk with almost anyone about God or faith. Bring the word Jesus or Christ into a conversation. If the person is not Christian you get the blank stares and again as I call it "the look" The look of disgust and like your feeding them poison. Friends and Family are not always supportive of you being a Christian. It's important to keep your faith but not destroy relationships with your non believing friends and family. I have friends that we might not talk to each other for years and as soon as we see each other we pick up right where we were in the past. I see that same pattern as being healthy for a non-believing friend or family member.

    As promised here is the brief story of John's conversion. While I was waiting for Jack and Alice to stop by I thought about my dad's friend named John. Shortly after 2010 I focused on a friend of the family member named John. Who I found out was dying. He was in an end of life hospice facility. Before then it had been maybe five years since I had last seen or talked with John. In the past I had talked to him and he had expressed that Christianity was just a crutch for weak people. He would say God is just made up. He said all the typical stuff a non-believer would say. When I came into the hospital room of John He was friendly as usual. He was a hard working successful business man. He was now in his early 70's. He was charming, yet he had joked about God many times. I wanted to make sure he was okay dying. I drove to the hospital he was in. I asked him point blank "What's going to you happen when you die? He said "nothing, you just cease to exist. Nothing happens, no Heaven, no Hell no God." I asked are you sure? He said yes smugly and smiled. He added "we all just evolved and there is no creator or God." "I asked again are you sure about all that?"I asked can I share some truth with you." He said "truth! There is no truth on these types of issues." I said well if there is no truth then how do you know what you believe is truth or just opinion. He smiled, chuckled a little and said "go ahead tell me what you want to say" I asked did you know there have been hundreds of thousands of NDE around the world? He asked what's a NDE? I answered "a Near Death Experience. Those are recorded incidents where someone was clinically dead and then latter they resuscitated. "Interesting" John said. I continued, "So these are documented, you can research them yourself. They all had the next thing in common. At death they all stated that they were aware and fully conscious of what was going on around them. Even though their body died, they had no breathing, heart function and no brain activity. It was as I like to say, like being in a car and then running out of gas or fuel. While in the car you can see what is happening but you no longer have any control over the car. It's dead. So you're thought of everything going dark and seeing nothing or experiencing nothing is not supported by eyewitnesses that have gone to the other side. This friend of the family smiled and titled his head. "Interesting, so none of these people experienced still, I guess nothingness? He asked. NO, I said not one person who died and came back said there was nothing.

John had for years talked about evolution discrediting a need for God. Next, I planned to discredit evolutionism. I had studied creation science for nearly 30 years. Yet getting a pro evolution thinking person to switch was a nearly

"Where are they now?"

impossible feat. John was a smart man and he would not change his mind on evolution with scripture. He needed science and logic to change his mind. Fortunately there is a truck load of science and logic on the side of special creation.
Now let's move onto the harder topic of evolution. I said. "That one is easy" he said "evolution is an established fact." I replied, "If I can discredit evolution with science and logic would that move you to accepting Christ? "Doing that is absolutely impossible, but give it your best shot kid, John chuckled. He was right he was 72 and I was 45, to him I was a kid. John had his facts ready to go. First I asked him how the world and universe started. He sat up in bed and proceeded with "well lightning hit some chemicals and the chemicals came alive." He was pleased with his own response. I said "did you know that in 1952 The Miller-Urey experiment ran for two weeks and was a failure. It proved that life does not come from non-life. He did not know that. He said "well then everything created itself." I told him if you had nothing as evolutionists believe then you would always have nothing. Something can't create itself. It has no ability to do so. He said what about all the cavemen? They prove we evolved. Sure I said let's talk about the Cavemen. I said did you know Lucy was discredited in 1981 by group of agnostic scientists? Did you know the Piltdown man was discredited in 1953 by a group of their piers? Did you know Peking man was discredited by a group of agnostic piers in 1972? John just stared at me. Then I continued, "Did you know Java man and Nebraska man were discredited by a group of agnostic scientific piers? Java man fell in 1985 and Nebraska man fell in 1930. John do you remember what

the definition of science is? "Yes science is observable and repeatable, so what?" So evolution is not observed and is not repeatable. Therefore it is not science. It is a belief. By this point John was a little deflated and a lot irritated. He said I can't change my mind this late in my life. I said sure you can you just don't want to. I said you can get right with God right now. To get right with him you just have to believe that God the father raised Christ from the dead. Only God the father can give you the faith to believe that. Jesus has paid the price for admittance to Heaven. You or I can never be good enough to have eternal life earned. Going to Heaven is a gift the wages are something we can never pay or come close to attaining. How could living perfect for 70 or 80 years earn a person eternity in Heaven? Heaven is for forgiven people, not perfect people. It's for those who are forgiven and who want a relationship with God. The relationship with God is the pinnacle for the Christian. God made it that way. God is the fuel we need to run on. God is our life. Our lives are hid in Christ. You can have that now before you die. After you die and have told God no thank you. God gives you what you asked for, an existence away from him and away from all that is good that he provides and that's literally everything. John was blankly looking at me. I asked do you want to be connected to God or spend forever by yourself away from him and everyone else. None of the people who died and had a Hellish experience partied or had any fellowship with others. It was complete darkness and isolation. There are no friends or beloved family to visit in Hell. If they are there you would never know. John said "I think this God stuff might be making since after all. "Good", I said "do you want to ask Christ to save you. Do you believe that

"Where are they now?"

Christ died as payment for your sins, and that the God the Father raised him from the dead?" Okay you have to believe it and say it out loud. About then a man taking the lunch time meal orders came in. My friend John said "I want the chicken lunch." Pausing a moment then John said I also want you to know I just accepted that Jesus died and was resurrected by his Father in Heaven. The man taking his order fist bumped John. He said "that great man, I'm a Christian myself. I'll go put your order in for lunch. Good job John, getting together with God will be the best part of your life." The guy walked out of the room. John said "I feel like something has changed". I told John if you have now believed and confessed that Jesus is Lord then the Holy Spirit will be now living along side of you. He will give you comfort. He takes away the terror that non-believers have about death. He will remind you of scriptures. You have to read the scripture in order for him to remind you of them. God will give you wisdom if you ask. Wisdom the Holy Spirit will give, God even gives wisdom to non-believers if they ask for it. "So what exactly is wisdom again?" asked John so God will give you insight on how to use the facts and knowledge you all ready have. The Holy Spirit can give you a word of knowledge that you did not know. John said "this is all very interesting, I'm also feeling a little overwhelmed. Can we pick this up another time? "Sure no problem" I said, "you're saved now" That is exciting" said now smiling John. "Come back in a day or two and tell me more." I said "sounds good." I added "Here is a copy of the new testament that I like. "Thanks" said John. With that I patted his arm and left his room. Two days later I got a call from my dad saying "your friend John died". I gave my dad a recap of what John and I had talked about. My dad said "yah I talked to him yesterday. My dad said "John said you came to visit and talk with him. He said he believes now that God is real. He believes that Jesus died and was resurrected. He said he feels God in the room with him." My dad continued, "For the years I knew John he had always said when you die there is nothing else. This was the first time where he acknowledged that God is real. He said he had to get saved in order to be in Heaven when he died. John told me you get saved by truly believing that Jesus died and was resurrected. Also you have to tell others you believe that. John called me and started telling me all this. I think he was converted. That God put his spirit in him. Like I said John never talked like that before. I really, truthfully believe that he was saved before he died. I wanted you to know, because I know you tried to lead him to Christ.

Thanks dad, Frank continued, John was tough he had chuckled for years if I brought up the words God or Jesus or salvation. On my way driving to the hospice hospital to see John, the Holy Spirit gave me some encouragement. You know how the Holy Spirit brings scripture to mind just at the right time you need. I had Jesus' word on it saying "don't be discouraged but be of good cheer; I have overcome the World.

"Dad I felt empowered to tell John the hard things about life and life after death. At first he blew me off as usual. Then I tore up and discredited his evolution nonsense and told him the time is 11:59 and you not ready for anything coming in your afterlife. From there we had a real discussion. He said the sinner's prayer and seemed legitimately changed and converted. My dad chimed in "John was always like a brother to me. I knew him as a young kid.

"Where are they now?"

You know you don't always have a lot of friends for 70 plus years." My dad was getting tired at the time my dad was 79 years old himself. My dad lived until 87. My own dad did not come to Christ until late in life. He was in mid 70's when he got serious about God.

I got off the phone with my dad. I then moved to my front yard swing. Out of the blue Jack's truck pulled up in front of my house. He got out and walked up my walkway. While he was still walking, out of the blue Alice pulled up. She got out of her Subaru and her two super cute Shiba Inu dogs leaped out and ran full speed to my front yard swing. They lick like crazy and act more like cats than dogs. Jack and Alice got up to my swing. They both said hay man we got to go check on the other nine. I said the other nine what? Jack said the rest of our soft ball team dummy. I said oh, Okay then let's go get them saved. They both said relax. I just stood there for a moment as they shook their heads at me. I patted my pocket and felt my car keys and I thought these two will just probably go in and visit with my wife and three daughters.

As I was thinking that, Jack and Alice walked in to the house. I could hear them making small talk. I thought this is my chance to go check on those nine. I slowly walked to my car. Started it and tried to drive away slowly. I heard Jack yell "Franks making a break for it." Before I know it six people were telling me to stop and then I heard them say let's go get him. In a moment they were following me over to one of the softball players' houses. It was Kevin; I had heard he was in the worst shape of the bunch. Pray he wants to hear and accept the Lord. For the Fame of Christ's name. Amen.

LAST WORDS

Here I am again; I hope you learned helpful, soul challenging and calming truths. Writing this story was something I almost did not do. My last short book about dealing with facts and faith surrounding the Titanic was slow in selling. It dealt quite a bit about dealing with death. In 2018, I began thinking I should write on what really actually happens after people die. For five years I ignored writing "Where are they now?" At the end here I want to have the hardest and scariest punch that I can deliver. This life, yours and my life are being lived in the presence of an invisible audience. Yah I know, that sounds like paranoia. Did you know at a micro level there is more that is un-seen than is seen. Whatever is surrounding you at this moment, at a molecular level there is literally more material down at a molecular level than you can even see. Even a hard table has more space between molecules than solid space. The same is true of the spirit world. God is watching you. We live in the same space as God exists in. It's very similar to your internet on your phone, or a radio or TV program on your television. As soon as you tune into a program or video or radio station you receive the signal. When a person prays God does not have to race across the universe to listen. He is literally with you.

No one other than God is omnipresent. But, there are fallen angels that want to blind you to this unseen spirit world. They don't tell you they are working very hard against you. They use and employ a couple of very effective strategies. One is they help a person get so wrapped up in themselves and any problems, that they give up looking to God. Or they think God is too far away or he doesn't exist at all. They get too busy. Fallen angels want humans to believe that God is not real. Or, that he God does not care about them individually.

Another part of the fallen angel's strategy is to run out the clock. This one works great for fallen angels and badly for us. If they can get humans to get and then stay wrapped up in problems and actives for their whole lives they have won. They just have to keep humans distracted until the game buzzer rings, AKA they die. Then the fallen angels have contributed to God losing another human. God does not actually misplace his human creation. Many humans keep God at arm's length.

Anyone that is still listening, hear this you have a real and present enemy of your life and soul. He and his followers hate God and you. If you can be a trophy for Lucifer, he will gladly bring you down to the sides of the pit. God has made a way of pardon for us all. Jesus came that we might have life and have it more abundantly. Don't let Lucifer's plans for you paralyze you and don't go to the other extreme of thinking, this is all garbage. Life and death

"Where are they now?"

happen at some point to us all. Waiting until after you die to learn about the afterlife is not smart. You are sealed away from God or with God at the moment of your death. Nothing you ever accomplish will ever be more important than taking care of what happens to you specifically one minute after you die. Be wise or chose to be foolish. The choice is 100% yours.

THE TRUTH WATERFALL

*I*n the beginning was the word and word was with God, and the Word was God. He was with God in the beginning. Through him all things were made. This word of God, the very expression of God is Christ Jesus.

—John 1

Jesus speaking; "If you have seen me you have seen the Father."

—John 14:9

Jesus speaking; I am the way, the truth and the life. No one comes to the Father except through me.

—John 14:6

No person can get into Heaven without Jesus letting you in. He has the keys of life Death and Hell's in his hands.

— Revelation 1:18

Jesus speaking; unless a man be born again he cannot see the kingdom of God.

— John 3:3

Jesus continuing; except a man (person) be born of water, (natural birth) and of the Holy Spirit, he cannot enter into the Kingdom of God.

— John 3:5

Only God brings the birth of the Holy Spirit. Which is God living in and along side of you. Only God births or creates the birth of the Holy Spirit. In the Greek the word Paraclete is used. The word means one who is alongside of you. (John 14:15-18) If you don't have that you are without God's fellowship in your life.

"*Where are they now?*"

Jesus speaking; I have come that you might have life and have it more abundantly.

—John 10:10

Jesus speaking: Truly, truly I tell you whoever hears my word and believes him who sent me HAS eternal life and will not be judged but has crossed over from death to life.

—John 5:24

Jesus speaking: I give them eternal life, and they shall never perish; no one will pluck them out of my hand.

—John 10:28

Jesus continuing: My father, which gave them to me is greater than all; and no man is able to pluck them out of my Father's hand.

—John 10:29

Jesus speaking on himself: He that believeth on him is not condemned: but he that believeth not is condemned already, because he hath not believed in the name of the only begotten Son of God.

—John 3:18

Jesus speaking: and whosoever liveth and believeth in me shall never die. Believest thou this?

—John 11:26

But to as many as received him, to them gave he power to become the sons of God, even to them that believe on his name: Which were born, not of blood, nor of the will of the flesh, nor of the will of man, but of God.

—John 1:12-13

Jesus speaking: He that believeth on the Son hath (present tense) everlasting life: and he that believeth not the Son shall not see life; but the wrath of God abides on him.

—John 3:36

"*Where are they now?*"

Jesus praying to the Father: Father, I desire that they also whom you have given Me, be with Me where I am, so that they may see My glory which you have given Me, for you loved Me before the foundation of the world.

—John 17:24

Jesus speaking: All that the Father gives me shall come to me; and him that cometh to me I will in no wise cast out.

—John 6:37

Jesus continuing: For I came down from Heaven, not to do mine own will, but the will of him that sent me. And this is the Father's will which hath sent me, that of all which he hath given me I should lose none, but should raise them up again at the last day. And this is also the will of him that sent me, that every one which sees the son, and believeth on him, may have everlasting life: and I will raise (resurrect their body) him up at the last day.

—John 6:38-40

Jesus speaking: I pray to the Father, and he shall give you another Comforter, that he may abide with you forever;

Even the Spirit of truth; whom the world cannot receive, because it sees him not, neither does it know him: but you know him; because he dwells with you and shall be in you.

— John 14:16-17

Jesus speaking: For whatsoever is born of God overcomes the world: and this is the victory that overcomes the world, even our faith.

— 1 John 5:4

Believe on the Lord Jesus Christ, and thou shall be saved, and your house.

— Act 16:31

"Where are they now?"

Jesus speaking: For by grace (undeserved favor) are you saved through faith; and not of yourselves: it is the gift of God:

Not of works, lest any man should boast.

— Ephesians 2:8-9

Not by works of righteousness which we have done, but according to his mercy he saved us, by the washing of regeneration, and making us new threw the Holy Spirit.

— Titus 3:5

Made in the USA
Las Vegas, NV
15 February 2025

17701144R10118